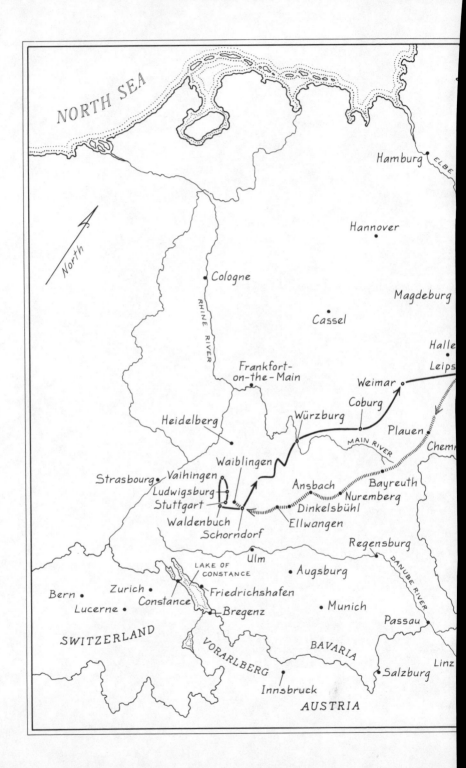

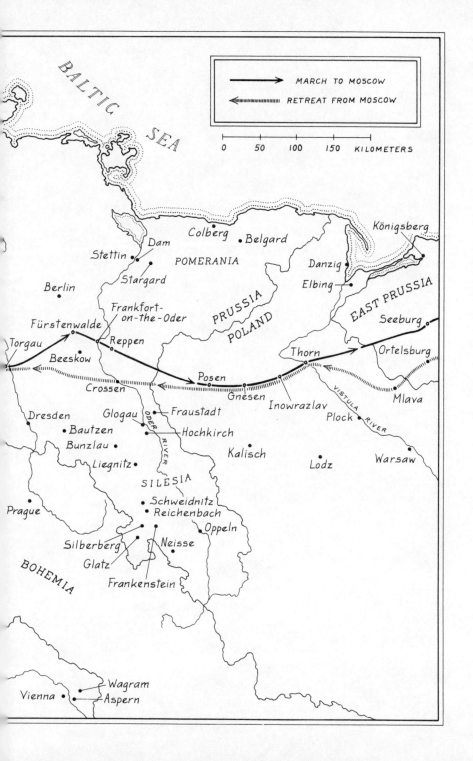

The Diary
of a
Napoleonic
Foot Soldier

JAKOB WALTER

Edited and with an Introduction

by Marc Raeff

Doubleday

New York London Toronto Sydney Auckland

The Diary

of a

Napoleonic

Foot Soldier

PUBLISHED BY DOUBLEDAY
a division of Bantam Doubleday Dell Publishing Group, Inc.
666 Fifth Avenue, New York, New York 10103

DOUBLEDAY and the portrayal of an anchor
with a dolphin are trademarks of Doubleday,
a division of Bantam Doubleday Dell Publishing Group, Inc.

Library of Congress Cataloging-in-Publication Data
Walter, Jakob, 1788–1864.
[Denkwurdige Geschichtschreibung über die erlebte
Millitäridienstzeit des Verfassers dieses Schreibens. English]
The diary of a Napoleonic foot soldier / Jakob Walter ; edited and
with an introduction by Marc Raeff. — 1st ed.
p.   cm.
Translation of: Denkwurdige Geschichtschreibung über die erlebte
Millitäridienstzeit des Verfassers dieses Schreibens.
Includes bibliographical references.
1. Walter, Jakob, 1788–1864.   2. Napoleonic Wars, 1800–1815—
Personal narratives, German.   3. Napoleonic Wars, 1800–1815—
Campaigns—Soviet Union.   4. Soldiers—Germany—Biography.
5. Germany. Heer—Biography.   I. Raeff, Marc.   II. Title.
DC226.5.W3513   1991
940.2'7—dc20   90-26735
                                                        CIP

ISBN 0-385-41696-2

Book design by Carol Malcolm-Russo

Copyright © 1991 by Doubleday
This edition was edited and prepared for publication by Marc Raeff

THE EDITOR WISHES TO THANK
VARTAN GREGORIAN,
WHO, AS PRESIDENT OF THE NEW YORK PUBLIC LIBRARY,
BROUGHT THIS MANUSCRIPT TO OUR ATTENTION.

GRATEFUL ACKNOWLEDGMENT IS MADE
TO EDWARD KASINEC,
CHIEF OF THE SLAVIC AND BALTIC DIVISION
OF THE NEW YORK PUBLIC LIBRARY,
FOR HIS INVALUABLE GUIDANCE.

Contents

Introduction

And us, the men, the mean, the
  rank and file?
Us, tramping broken, wounded,
  muddy, dying?
Having no hope of duchies and
  endowments. . . .

(ADAPTED INTO ENGLISH BY L. N. PARKER,
NEW YORK 1900)

Et nous, les petits, les obscurs, les
  sans-grades,
Nous qui marchions fourbus, blessés,
  crottés malades,
Sans espoir de duchés ni
  de dotations . . .

EDMOND ROSTAND,
L'AIGLON, ACTE II, SCÈNE 9

THE FRENCH REVOLU-
tion of 1789 seemed to many the
dawn of a new era—of a new world
order based on individual political
and economic freedoms. On the
other hand, Napoleon's rule
(1799–1815), which emerged from
the Revolution, struck his subjects
like a conquering whirlwind which came near to estab-
lishing France as the sole great power in the Western
world. True, Napoleon's reign was not only one of war
and conquest, it also helped to disseminate and to root
the "Rights of Man and of the Citizen" in many parts of
Europe, initiating a process of liberalization and democ-
ratization that is the foundation of our own times. All
this we see now, in retrospect—to contemporaries it must
have appeared differently. As we all know, profound social
and political transformations exact a heavy price from
those who benefit as well as from those who suffer from
them, while military conquests are bought with "blood,
sweat, and tears." The heroic saga of Napoleon's wars,
and the many victories won by his armies, reaped a boun-
tiful harvest of pride and glory for France; they are
celebrated by monuments, sung by poets, exalted by historians and national myths. Even while the legacy of
Napoleon recedes farther and farther from today's reality,

France and the world are about to celebrate the bicentennial of his deeds—witness the new *Dictionnaire Napoléon*, the refurbishing of monuments and museums to his glory, the staging of Edmond Rostand's paean, *L'Aiglon*, the exhibitions of the arts and artifacts of his times.

While we may recall Napoleon's glory and his genuinely lasting accomplishments in law, education, and administration—both in France and in vassal regions of Western and Central Europe—we cannot forget the price paid by his contemporaries, especially the little folk, the ordinary soldiers whose blood, sweat, and toil won his battles and brought him glory. The sad truth, however, is that the common people leave few historical records, whether written or material. We are particularly fortunate when ordinary fighting men, soldiers and noncommissioned officers, leave memoirs and autobiographies recounting their part in the Napoleonic epic. There are not many of them and we should be particularly keen to preserve the few we have and to make them widely known. This is the reason for republishing an English translation of one of the very rare autobiographies by an ordinary conscript soldier, and a German at that, who had the misfortune of participating in the disastrous campaign Napoleon undertook in the vain belief that he could defeat Russia. In addition we are fortunate to publish, for the first time in English, six letters written home by soldiers in the course of the campaign itself.

For over twenty years France was at war, involving at one time or another virtually all European states. Unlike all previous European wars, even those that had lasted for decades, the revolutionary and Napoleonic campaigns were fought by conscripts drawn from the general population; in a true sense they were the first "national wars" that involved practically the whole people. It has been estimated that in the course of fifteen years (1800–15) Napoleon raised about 2 million conscripts in France alone—about 7 percent of the total population. Little wonder that population growth in France fell dramatically, resulting in a relative decline of its population throughout the nineteenth century, at a time when England, Germany, and Prussia were having their largest population explosion ever.

Originally, "the nation in arms" had risen to defend the Revolution against the threat of a royalist restoration and of the elimination of the social and civic rights secured in 1789. It did not matter that, in point of fact, it was the revolutionary government that had declared war to forestall the coalition of Austria, Prussia, Russia, and England. The very success of France in driving back the armies of the monarchical alliance from its soil, and in pursuing them beyond the borders, created the conditions for a messianic drive to carry the message of liberation from the old order beyond what—since Richelieu's times—had been claimed as the "natural frontiers" of France, and the installation of "sister republics"—Batavian, in today's Belgium, Helvetian, Cisalpine in northern Italy, etc. Although it defeated its Continental enemies, republican France could not subdue England, whose implacable enmity (under the leadership of Pitt the Younger) precluded the recognition and security of the changes, both domestic and foreign, wrought by the Revolution since 1789. At least, this is the way it was seen and interpreted at the time by both sides. England would not acquiesce to French control of the estuary of the Rhine and of the Belgian coast, and continued to organize and subsidize Continental coalitions against France. In addition, Pitt and his government believed that a reinvigorated France might pose a threat to England's colonial empire and trade routes, especially in the eastern Mediterranean. Their belief seemed to be confirmed in 1798 by General Bonaparte's attempt to conquer Egypt and the coast of what is today Syria and Lebanon and to disrupt England's Eastern trade. Bonaparte's rhetoric (and aborted negotiations with Emperor Paul I of Russia) about striking at England in India did not contribute to making English policy more accommodating and pacific. As a result, all treaties of peace concluded between France and the other powers in the last decade of the eighteenth and the first years of the nineteenth centuries proved to be only truces to be broken at the first opportunity.

Napoleon had seized power to extricate France from the domestic difficulties that had been brought about by the mismanagement of the Directory, to consolidate the gains of the Revolution, and to enhance its—as well as his own—glory, by securing, and if possible expanding, the territorial acquisitions of the new French social and political order. Such a double goal could not but bring about a self-fulfilling prophecy of ever renewed coalitions and wars, and new territorial conquests stubbornly rejected by England. Napoleon succeeded in defeating Austria, Prussia, and Russia—but Nelson's victory at

Trafalgar precluded any serious French naval challenge and ensured that England would fight on and subsidize Continental allies, so that Napoleon never achieved the military and diplomatic security he craved. Napoleon's military genius brought victory and ever new conquests on the Continent, and war lasted, with short-term breathing spells, from 1799 to his failure in Russia in 1812 and final defeat in 1814–15.

In 1806, following the defeat of the Third Coalition at Austerlitz, the Holy German Empire of the Germanic Nation—in existence since the tenth century—was dissolved by its Emperor, Francis II, who was also ruler of the Habsburg lands. In its stead Napoleon created the Confederation of the Rhine, which in fact was a French satellite, encompassing the German states, with the exclusion of Austria and Prussia. The major states of the Confederation, Württemberg and Westphalia, were promoted to kingdoms—Württemberg keeping its ruler, while Westphalia, a new creation carved out from former sovereign principalities and Prussian lands, received as king Napoleon's younger brother Jérôme. Most important in our context, the various states of the Confederation had to furnish troops to be raised through a system of conscription similar to that of France. In the war of 1807–9 against Austria, Prussia, and Russia, contingents from these newly created kingdoms—promised significant territorial benefits after victory—fought on the side of the French. The author of our autobiography, Jakob Walter, had his first military experiences during that war.

Since he could not beat England by naval and military means, Napoleon tried to strangle it economically.

He proclaimed the Continental Blockade (Decree of Berlin, 21 November 1806) that prohibited all his satellites and allies from trading with England. After practically dismembering Prussia in 1807, Napoleon forced Alexander I, Emperor of Russia, to accept peace (treaty of Tilsit, 8 July 1807) and to join the Continental Blockade. Disagreements about the implementation of the blockade regulations constituted a major element of friction between Napoleon and Russia. This was exacerbated by serious discord over Poland. Emperor Alexander I considered control over neighboring Poland an essential element of his empire's security. On the other hand, Napoleon expected to use Poland as a friendly satellite to keep Prussia and Russia in check. He set up the Grand Duchy of Warsaw as an autonomous state, broadly hinting that it would serve as the nucleus of a revived Polish state under French tutelage. However, it was dawning on Napoleon that his domination over Continental Europe would never be secure as long as Russia, with its vast manpower resources and territory, was not cowed into submission. Only then, Napoleon fancied, could he force England, barred from all trade with Europe, to accept his peace terms.

Alexander I understood the situation just as well. Moreover, Russian court circles and economic interests found membership in the Continental Blockade highly onerous. Alexander I also realized that for all his promises, Napoleon would not give him a free hand against Turkey (with whom he was at war). When Napoleon came to the conviction that he had not obtained Alexander's genuine acceptance of his new order in Europe, he began preparing for a war against Russia. But he was quite aware that in order to defeat Russia decisively he would need an overwhelming force. He started to build up the Grande Armée in 1811 in preparation for the campaign against Russia. He hoped that, as had always been the case, a decisive victory at the start would compel Alexander I to sue for peace. His strategic plans, as well as the logistic preparation of the campaign, were predicated on the notion that war was but another instrument to achieve political ends. But, as is well known, the decisive battle eluded Napoleon. He was forced to push on into Russia's heartland, occupy Moscow, overextend his supply lines, and exhaust his troops. Yet, the Russian army remained at full strength and no peace offer was forthcoming from Alexander I. The burning of Moscow (whose true causes have still not been fully elucidated) proved to be the last straw and forced Napoleon to order the retreat. His exhausted troops, incapable of breaking through to the south (battle of Maloiaroslavets, 24 October 1812) to seek rest and supplies in the Ukraine, had to retrek on the road of invasion through a devastated countryside, prey to partisan attacks, and decimated by the hardships of a Russian winter, compounded by demoralization and famine. The star of Napoleon's power and glory was setting.

The revolutionary armies had been manned practically by Frenchmen only. But as Napoleon's empire expanded, and embroiled him into more and more wars, he came to call upon the populations of annexed and "allied" countries to contribute to the manpower needs of his army. Before 1812 he had called upon Italians and Germans to fight in campaigns near their own homeland, as our author documents in the first chapters of his autobiography. For the invasion of Russia, Napoleon again ordered conscription in all the states directly under his control. His Grande Armée in 1812 numbered about 600,000 men, of whom only about one half were French conscripts, while the remainder were made up of soldiers from Poland (the largest number, since the Poles hoped to regain their independence after a French victory), Italy, Holland, Austria, Prussia, and the states of the Confederation of the Rhine, more particularly Württemberg and Westphalia.

Following the French example, the German states, too, had introduced conscription. In Württemberg men between the ages of eighteen and forty were subject to conscription, active service being for eight years in the infantry and ten years in the cavalry and artillery. Thus, our hero Jakob Walter was first conscripted in 1806 and then recalled to duty twice, in 1809 and 1812. When Napoleon decided on the campaign against Russia he demanded that his German "allies," in fact satellites, mobilize too. In a letter, dated 27 January 1812, to Frederick, whom he had made king of Württemberg in 1806, he ordered that the Württemberg contingent be ready to march on 15 February 1812. The king had no alternative but to execute this order. Likewise, Napoleon's brother, King Jérôme of Westphalia, was ordered to furnish 27,000 men. Württemberg mobilized nine infantry regiments, as well as some artillery and cavalry units. The troops, 12,000 men in all, were placed under the nominal command of the Crown Prince William and were part of the corps commanded by Marshal Ney.

Napoleon's motives and policies are well documented and have been thoroughly analyzed, even though historians continue to disagree on a final assessment. But what made all his numerous conscripts fight on and on? First of all, naturally, compulsion and fear of retribution in case of disobedience and desertion. Although, as the years of war dragged on, and the burden of monetary contributions and conscription became increasingly heavy, the number of desertions and self-mutilations, to escape army service, grew by leaps and bounds. Nevertheless, in the case of the Frenchmen, revolutionary fervor and the magic of Napoleon's name, pride in the victories and the glory that rebounded on them—all served to sustain their energies in the hope of final victory and final reward. These attitudes are well documented in the memoirs of such French veteran soldiers as Sergeant Bourgogne and Captain Coignet, although one should make allowance for retrospective embellishments and anachronistic perspectives.

Unfortunately, there seem to be no equivalent sources for the Russian side. Although there is a vast documentation on the invasion of Russia and the subsequent campaigns of 1813–15, and an extensive historiography of this period of Russian history, there is practically nothing on and by the common soldier, as illustrated by most recent bibliographies of memoirs, letters, and autobiographies published in the Soviet Union. What there is comes in the form of some eyewitness accounts by merchants and artisans of the French occupation of Moscow and of its burning; as well as descriptions, collected by someone else, of a few peasants' and soldiers' experiences as members of the militia and partisan groups in 1812. This state of affairs is witness, on the one hand, to the comparatively low level of literacy of the Russian population (as compared with that of the ordinary peasant, town dweller, and soldier in France or the Germanies). On the other hand, it may also illustrate the greater reluctance of the Establishment and of the elites (in spite of their alleged populism) to let the common man speak for himself and the constrictive censorship instituted by Alexander I at the end of the war and reinforced, after 1825, by his successor Nicholas I. The relaxation of censorship after 1861 came too late to permit collecting materials that would not be overly distorted by a great chronological gap.

As in the case of the Poles, the Russians conceived of the campaign of 1812 as a war of liberation. For the former it held out the promise of liberation from foreign rule and the restoration of an independent Polish state— no wonder that Prince Poniatowski's corps performed particularly well until his death in battle at Leipzig in 1813. As for the latter, it was a truly defensive and allegedly patriotic war to safeguard the Orthodox faith and the integrity of the national way of life and territory. At the start of the war there had been concern in high places about the loyalty of the peasant-serfs in the western provinces and near Moscow. This concern, as well as stategic considerations, led the Russian command to adopt a policy of mass evacuation and scorched earth. Napoleon's failure to manifest any intention of freeing the serfs and to improve their lot (the same mistake Hitler was to repeat a century and a quarter later), and the ruthless pillage by his troops, turned even the most wretched Russian serf against the invader. Difficult as it is to accept the hagiographic clichés of popular enthusiasm in defense of the fatherland, there is no question that the Russian peasant did resist the invaders, and contributed his share to the French Emperor's defeat. The militia raised by the government and by private landowners surely took active part in exhausting and pursuing the Grande Armée.

None of this pertained to the German soldiers, whatever their state of origin. They shared neither French glories nor Polish and Russian patriotism. True, given the opportunity—and it was to present itself in 1813— the German elites, especially in Prussia, gladly rose against the French to recover their national dignity and sovereignty. In the meantime, however, they had to serve in the Grande Armée; but they did so without enthusiasm or any sense of the possible advantages to be gained from obediently fighting under Napoleon's command.

In the memoirs, autobiographies, and letters of ordinary soldiers from Germany, such as our main author Jakob Walter, we find total indifference as to the outcome of the campaign—only the hope of returning quickly and safely home, of surviving the hardships and the dangers that had fallen to their lot. Theirs is, therefore, a relatively "objective" picture of the Polish and Russian countryside and its conditions—and it is a dismal one. They do not really care who wins in battle or engagement: ready to assist each other, they are not interested either in killing more Russians or helping their fellow soldiers of other nationalities. They are not vengeful or spiteful, either—in spite of the sufferings that Napoleon, French rule, and the Russians visit upon them; theirs is what the French call *égoïsme sacré*, a healthy drive to survive. To escape hunger and avoid disease are their main concerns, and this is what frequently transforms them into callous brutes.

To understand Jakob Walter's autobiography and the letters by Westphalian soldiers better, we should say a few words about the way in which Napoleon's armies were supplied and equipped. One of the great achievements of Napoleon as military commander, besides his strategic and tactical talents, had been his skill in organizing the mobility and logistic support of his troops. As he relied heavily on artillery and the firepower of his highly maneuverable infantry and cavalry, he paid particular attention to the ready availability of guns and small firearms, as well as of an adequate supply of ammunition. He also made sure that his engineers had the wherewithal to build pontoon bridges and lay siege to fortresses. Given the primitive technology of transportation, one that relied almost exclusively on horsepower and manpower, few resources were left for an efficient system to bring food and clothing to the troops. Thus regular pay had as its main purpose to enable individual soldiers to turn to the civilian market for their additional needs. Clothing was issued at more or less regular intervals and, by and large, in sufficient quantity and of acceptable quality for normal conditions of war; although no serious effort was made to adapt the clothing to the climatic conditions of specific campaigns.

As for foodstuffs, under "normal" circumstances, a minimum quantity of bread was supplied by regimental bakeries. Practically everything else, and naturally in situations where the field bakeries could not be moved on time close enough to the fighting men, had to be obtained on the spot. The local population was compelled to furnish shelter (through billeting) and food, through requisitions by units detached for that purpose by the commander. Additional food—and liquor, of course—was to be purchased either from local traders or from sutlers (canteen keepers) who accompanied the regiments; many sutlers were women, frequently the wives of professional noncoms and soldiers. In Central and Western Europe, areas that were densely populated and, on the whole, quite prosperous, with an elaborate network of traders and stores, this "system" worked fairly well. Especially when it was supplemented by marauding—forbidden, of course, but tolerated as long as it was not excessive. In this respect, the Württemberg soldiers had a particularly bad record, as Walter illustrates.

Inherited by the Revolution and Napoleon from the practice of the standing armies introduced after the Thirty Years' War, this "system" would not work as expected in areas too poor to have any kind of surplus, or emptied of their population and of everything edible and movable. This, however, was precisely the situation that the Grande Armée encountered when it crossed into Russian Poland and from there into Russia proper. Russian Poland was poor, with a sparse population and an extremely backward agrarian economy that provided barely enough sustenance to avoid permanent hunger. Trade networks were primitive, too—peddlers and small village stores (mostly operated by Jews) carried only a few items of necessity and shoddy luxuries. Conditions in Russia were even worse. The Byelorussian provinces that lay between eastern Poland and Moscow were among the poorest in European Russia: swamps, forests, and a few tilled fields bearing a poor crop of rye. Here, too, there were a meager number of inhabitants, settled in widely scattered villages; manor houses and noble estates were also few and far between, and far from magnificent. The situation was made worse for the Grande Armée by two developments: first, scare propaganda and direct orders of the Russian authorities had resulted in the mass flight of the local population; second, the Russian armies, as they retreated, destroyed everything that could be remotely of use to the enemy—crops, stores of grain, fodder, and hay, cattle, and even peasant dwellings (setting whole villages afire). That is why, from the start of the campaign, Napoleon's troops lacked food supplies; the situation grew worse as the Grande Armée advanced deeper into the empire, and it became tragically catastrophic on the retreat. Whatever supplies could be secured by headquarters went first to the French troops, in particular the Imperial Guard; soldiers of the vassal states were left to their own devices.

Napoleon's attempt at subduing Russia ended in tragic disaster, signaling the beginning of his doom. Of about 600,000 men who crossed into Russia in June 1812, about 140,000 retreated from Moscow, and barely 25,000 recrossed the border in December 1812. The disaster triggered the uprising for national liberation in Prussia and the renewal of an all-European coalition against France. Alexander I's decision—against the advice of his commander in chief, Marshal M. I. Kutuzov—to continue fighting after the expulsion of the Grande Armée from his realm, eventually led to Napoleon's defeat and exile, the entrance of the allies into Paris, and the return of King Louis XVIII to the throne of his ancestors. Little wonder that the campaign of Russia appeared to be proof of Napoleon's *hybris* and, as in Greek classical tragedy, conjured up his own *nemesis*. In Victor Hugo's words, *on était conquis par sa conquête* (one was conquered by one's conquest).

The tragic end of Napoleon's epic has generated an immense literature, for it offered the dramatic contrast of almost superhuman triumphs and glory followed by an abyss of misery and wretchedness. It is the image of the Napoleonic legend which the emperor created and fostered with the help of his chamberlin in exile, Las Cases, who published the vastly popular *Mémorial de Sainte-Hélène*, an "oral history" of Napoleon's spoken reminiscences. It was kept alive by the stirrings of nationalism and liberalism in France, as well as in the rest of Europe. The legend also owed much to the fact that the revolutionary and Napoleonic armies had helped to spread the political notions and the social legislation that were the hallmark of modern democratic civil and economic freedoms. The digruntled demobilized soldiers and noncoms of his armies were the living illustration of Napoleon's magnetic appeal and titanic figure, both of which the songs of Béranger and the poetry of Heine, Hugo, Lermontov, and others popularized throughout Europe.

It is no exaggeration to say that the tragic campaign of 1812 did more than anything else to bring about the birth of a modern national consciousness in Russia and the Germanies. In Russia, it was the pride of having been the first in defeating the mighty military genius of Napoleon. The military leadership and the selfless patriotism of the people had been the instruments of this defeat, and thus had given proof of Russia's having come of age to save European civilization. This interpretation held sway throughout the imperial regime until 1917 and it was revived on the eve of the Second World War by Stalin; it has not been seriously challenged or amended to this day in Soviet historiography. As far as the Germans were concerned, the French conqueror's defeat made possible an uprising when the Prussian General Yorck von Wartenburg initiated a war of national liberation from the French; it became an all-German uprising when volunteers, mainly students and burghers, from the other states flocked to participate in the so-called *Freiheitskrieg* (War of Liberation) of 1813–15. This war came to symbolize the emergence of an all-German national consciousness that demanded the creation of a unitary German state. As we know, it served as prelude and justification for Bismarck's drive to unite Germany, minus Austria, into one empire under the unchallenged dominance of Prussia. The Second Reich, replacing the first, the Holy Roman Empire of the Germanic Nation, lasted until 1918; a German unitary state, exclusive of Austria,

existed until 1945 and, at the present, has reemerged
again.

Jakob Walter's autobiography chronicles only what
he witnessed and experienced himself. There is no place
in it for general reflections, no effort is made to explain
or interpret the wars in which he was involved. This is
so despite the fact that he apparently wrote decades after
the events and quite clearly, as Frank E. Melvin's commentary (which in this volume follows Walter's diary)
shows, reconstructed details of the campaign with the
help of maps and published histories. Walter has no other
ambition than to record, as faithfully as he can, the events
in which he himself took part; he has no ulterior motives,
no moral or other judgments in mind. He merely testifies
to the beastliness that may surface in every man under
conditions of extreme hardship and in fear of one's life.
What is also quite remarkable, I think, he displays no
bitterness either toward Napoleon and the French, nor
toward the Russian enemies. On the other hand, there is
no sign of any emotional involvement in the events. His
autobiography is as objective a chronicle as one can get,
moreover a chronicle from the rare perspective of a lowly
soldier, foreign to Napoleon's and French interests and
concerns. It is written exclusively for home consumption,
to tell the immediate family and their descendants how
one of their own fared in those turbulent times. This is,
of course, equally true of the letters we reproduce later
in the book—except that they convey facts and feelings
on the spot, in the very midst of military action.

The text of Jakob Walter's autobiography is reproduced, with minor corrections, from the translation first published in *Bulletin of the University of Kansas—Humanistic Studies*, vol. VI, no. 3 (Lawrence, Kans.: University of Kansas, Department of Journalism Press), 1938, under the title *A German Conscript with Napoleon—Jakob Walter's Recollections of the Campaigns of 1806–1807, 1809, and 1812–1813*, edited and translated by Otto Springer (professor of Germanic Languages) with historical collaboration by Frank E. Melvin (associate professor of History).

We are reproducing, omitting unnecessary rhetoric and detail, the historical commentary and notes of Frank E. Melvin. It was deemed unneccessary, for this edition, to reproduce the philological notes and commentary on Walter's language by Otto Springer, the original editor and translator.

In the present edition the text of the translation has been rearranged so that the order of the chapters follows the chronological sequence of events. The illustrations, which are contemporary with the manuscript, have been selected with the help of Edward Kasinec, Chief of the Slavic and Baltic Division of the New York Public Library, from the holdings of that division and the permission of the Trustees of the Library.

—Marc Raeff
September 1990

PORTRAIT OF JAKOB WALTER AT THE AGE OF FIFTY.

The Diary

of a

Napoleonic

Foot Soldier

MEMORABLE HISTORY OF THE MILITARY SERVICE
EXPERIENCED BY THE AUTHOR OF
THIS TEXT

Campaign

of

1806 and 1807

IN THE YEAR 1806, I WAS drafted with many of my comrades into military service in the conscription at that time and was assigned to the regiment of Romig, which afterward was given the name of Franquemont and of Number 4 and which was in the Ludwigsburg garrison. In the fall I traveled with the regiment to Prussia in the campaign which Emperor Napoleon with the princes, then his allies, was conducting at that time against Prussia. In the fall we marched through Ellwangen, Nuremberg, Ansbach, Bayreuth, Plauen, Dresden in Saxony, then through Bunzlau into Grossglogau in Silesia, where we remained in garrison for about three weeks.

During a period from the month of January to the month of March, I had to go with half of the regiment to accompany several convoys of captured Prussians from Glogau back through Crossen, Frankfort-on-the-Oder, and Dresden, where we were relieved. We were given good quarters everywhere, which kept me always healthy and cheerful in spite of the continuous marching. Furthermore, I was only nineteen years old, a fact which caused me frequently to participate in thoughtless and dangerous enterprises. During our return to Glogau the convoy, together with a Bavarian corps, was surrounded by Prussians in Bunzlau. We then closed all the gates and caught the spies.

In this city it happened in my quarter that a comrade wanted to force the landlord to sing. However, he refused to do so, sitting the whole night on a bench near the stove weeping. Since this man could not sing because of his sorrow, Soldier Hummel wanted to frighten him, took his rifle, cocked the hammer, and shot. The bullet passed by me and another soldier and lodged in the wall. I wanted to mention this in order to show how the soldiers were running wild at that time.

A spy who was a village smith was brought before the guard house. He had letters and orders to tell the Prussians of our strength in man power. He was laid on a bench and whipped by two or three corporals. Two men had to hold his feet and two his head. His leather breeches were stretched out and water poured on them, and then he received about one hundred and fifty blows. At last he could no longer speak, because he was half dead. At every blow the lieutenant said to the smith, "This is a Bavarian thaler; this is a Württemberg thaler," at which the lieutenant was really able to laugh. After this experience the smith was taken to the threshing floor [?] and shot. Blows with clubs also were heaped upon many innocent people in this city.

When the Prussians who were laying siege to the city lost their courage, they withdrew, and we entered Glogau again.

After I had been in Glogau one day, I had to escort with a part of the regiment 19 money wagons to the

Grand Army. These money wagons were drawn by four and six horses, and many sank into the mire every day. This march went through Breslau and then across the Polish border to Kalisch, Posen, Gnesen, [Inowr]azlav, and Thorn on the Vistula River, where the convoy was given over. From there we had to return to Gnesen, a sizable city in Poland. There we had a storeroom to guard, watching in a room at a bright fire. In this house there was a Polish soldier's wife who taught me as much Polish as I would need. We suffered from the cold a great deal there during the two weeks of our stay because our feet got no warmth and a severely cold winter prevailed.

Finally, eight men, including myself, were sent into the outlying villages by the Commandant of the city. I received several written orders to requisition food supplies; yet, even though I did not know the roads, I was

1. Pencil sketch by Eberhard Emminger of Walter's home city of Ellwangen, dated 1847.

not furnished with a guide. Since I had to carry out my commission, I went, as did my other comrades, into the Jewish section, where everyone spoke German but few could read or write it and few, as I found out, could read Polish. There I wanted to take the first Jew I came across as a guide, but the first escaped and likewise the others I chased. Finally, I ran after one and chased him into the attic of his house and caught him among many women and children. Here he wanted to defend himself, and I had to use force. I took him, dragged him down the two flights of stairs, and had to hold him by the coat and kick him forward for two hours, threatening him if he should fail to lead me to the right village. Here I had to walk through a lake, and the water went over my knees. I commanded the Jew to lead the way, and he howled so loudly for fear of drowning that I had to laugh and send him back immediately. After crossing, the Jew sat down and shook out his water-filled boots.

After I arrived in the village ahead of me, the nobleman quartered me in the mayor's house; but, when I entered the room through a straw door, I could not stand upright and could not see any people for the smoke. This compelled me to quarter myself at the nobleman's house.

The next day I tried to visit eight villages, but I frequently got to only one or two in a day, for often it was necessary to walk a distance of three or four miles. In one manor I once could get no guide, since everyone ran away and hid from my lone self. A big dog also kept attacking me, and I shot the dog because of my customary youthful impulses. This was another reason why I got no guide. Here I traveled alone, depending upon my own good judgment, to a village in another region and received here, as almost everywhere, unrequested presents which pleased me very much.

Since, as I have said, it required eight days insted of four to visit the villages and since the convoy lying in Gnesen left hurriedly, I and three other men returned too late. The convoy was gone. Having obtained the route of march from Gnesen to the Neisse stronghold in Silesia, we had to march alone a distance of about one hundred hours.

Since we four men thought we were well off, we did not hurry to catch the convoy but contented ourselves with comfortable traveling. We visited the noblemen, who usually had to hitch up their own good horses for us while we threatened that we had to catch the convoy by the next day and that the noblemen could be made responsible if we missed it. However, we usually had to combine force with these methods to get horses.

Once we took four horses from a nobleman, and unfortunately the march led us through a large govern-ment city, Posen. Here the servant said something we could not understand to a few burghers, but we were not stopped. We wanted to drink some brandy in the last suburb, and we halted. At once the nobleman came up on a white horse, being a Polish general stationed there in garrison. Our position did not seem to be the best, and we had to discuss what was to be done. Quickly our sickest-looking comrade had to lie on the ground and continually moan and lament. The general greeted us by threatening to write to our headquarters in Silesia about such use of his horses. That might have happened if the sick man had not aroused some serious doubt on the part of the general. To defend ourselves further, we said we had just as much right to complain to our regiment that His Excellency the general had hindered our progress and had caused the death of a sick man. At these words a wagon with two horses was brought there at once, and we were able to travel away laughing with our healthy "sick man."

After Posen we came into a little Polish town called Fraustadt, which was a garrison town. I have to mention this town because of its windmills, which numbered 99.

From Fraustadt we came after several marches to Glogau on Easter Eve and were quartered with a Jew. Since we were acquainted in this city, we wanted to give this Jew something to remember us by. The meals were usually attended by violence on account of stinginess and uncleanliness; and, since clean chinaware was always set up for the Jews, we took over all that chinaware and ate with it, causing such an uproar in the house that a crowd of people gathered in front of the house to listen. Our defense was that we just had not thought of making anything unkosher that had been intended not to be for us, and so the Jews could not set forth any complaint.

From Glogau we traveled with some of the Black Riflemen toward the stronghold of Schweidnitz. We had not obtained a wagon out of Glogau, which seemed to us a great hardship. It was Easter Day, March 29, and we looked for horses in every stable in a village called Hochkirch, but found none, which failure made it necessary for us to look even in the parsonage.

When we searched the buildings and found nothing

but an old woman there, we wanted to look into the church where the service was in progress, and we found the church full of people. Meanwhile there stood in the court a beautiful carriage hitched with two horses; so we untied the horses and rode away without a servant. Since we had to hurry to escape the church folk, I had to drive and ran into a tree stump so that the carriage and all of us lay there in the mud. Here we set out again and traveled until we were a half mile from Schweidnitz. In that place there was a tavern in the forest; and, after we had sold the carriage and horses cheaply to the innkeeper, we continued our march.

When we came to the fortress of Neisse, we had to go on with our regiment and with the Seckendorff Regiment through Breslau, across Poland through the city of Kalisch, then Posen, Gnesen, [Inowr]azlav, and Thorn on the Vistula River. From there we went through Prussian Pomerania toward the fortress of Colberg on the Baltic Sea. One mile from this stronghold is a town called Belgard, and ther was a castle there which had belonged to our King Frederick while he had encamped in this town as general of the cavalry.

On this journey from Thorn to Colberg I saw a lake which lay in a forest by a monastery. In this lake were multitudes of frogs which were of a very beautiful bright blue color, and no soldier would quit until he had caught one of these beautiful frogs. Beyond this region we came to a little town in which the largest part of the inhabitants were Jews. The same day we had had to walk several miles through swamps and snow water up to our knees; and, when quarters were taken there for the evening, I and four other men came into a Jew's house. The room was full of straw and goats. Since neither fire nor wood was to be had, we went into the next house to lodge, looked for the Jew, and took him into custody; for only by applying such stern treatment could we induce the wife to bring us food on her husband's account.

While we were besieging the fortress of Colberg, we were assigned a camp in a swampy place. Since wood and even straw were rarely to be had, the barracks were built from earth and sod, and ditches were dug around them.

As some sickness was arising because of the continual fog, I also became sick and had to go to the hospital in the fortress of Stettin, which is also a fortress on the sea. When I arrived with several from the regiment, we were placed three stories high under the roof in the hospital. Here twelve to fifteen of the men about me died every day, which made me sick at my stomach and would have caused my death in the end if I and four comrades had not reported ourselves as being well even on the second day and escaped. This hospital and three others, according to rumor, had six thousand sick people; and that was the reason also why everyone with an appetite had to suffer great hunger, which was one of the things that moved me to leave. The third day we five men were allowed to go, and we traveled without delay to our regiment.

In this fortress of Stettin the Würzburg soldiers were stationed and were all dressed in uniforms of white and red, that is, like Austrian soldiers. This stronghold had a position which could be besieged only by land from the side facing Berlin. Here the Oder River flows into the Baltic Sea. This, together with the swamps, which extend for a mile and through which currents of the Oder flow, surrounds two-thirds of the city. Over the swamp is a paved dike a mile long, reaching to the head of the bridge near a village named Dam. This city is large and beautiful and had especially large merchant ships in the harbor to look at.

When we five men came again without delay to the fortress of Colberg, we had the honor of enduring the siege in good health for another three weeks. Pentecost Night is especially fixed in my memory, since the fortress was stormed then.

When we had to leave camp after midnight, all the regiments marched forward through the swamp; and finally, when light firing began upon the outposts, we were commanded to attack by wading through the rampart ditches with fascines, to tread these in, and to scramble up the outworks by chopping and shoveling. When I stood in the ditch, each first soldier had to pull up the next one with his rifle. The ramparts were of sand, and everyone frequently fell back again because of the attack of the enemy, or just because of the sliding sand; yet in that place the huge cannonballs flew by above us [?], thundering so violently that we would have believed the earth would burst to pieces. When everyone was almost on top of the earthwork, the Prussians were slaughtered with great vigor, and the rest took flight into the gate. Then we, too, wanted to gain possession of the gateway in order to enter the city, but at this critical time many of these Prussians were shot along with our men by small and large guns, and the gate was closed.

Since all sorts of shells and rockets broke out of the fortress like a cloudburst, we had to take to flight. Those who meanwhile were scrambling up the outworks had to jump from the fortress into the moat along with their prisoners, and all the rest had to do likewise. During this retreat many fell on bayonets, many drowned, and many of us were also brought into the fortress as prisoners and sent away to Danzig by sea.

When we reached camp, we saw many who had lost their helmet, rifle, saber, knapsack, etc. Because of various falls and pains, many looked for wounds and had none;

2. *WATERCOLOR BY AN UNKNOWN ARTIST OF THE PALACE SQUARE IN STUTTGART, ABOUT 1790.*

many, however, did not become aware of the wounds which they had until they reached camp.

In this camp there were Poles, Westphalians, French, and, as mentioned before, only two regiments of us from Württemberg. One morning the Prussians surprised the Polish camp from the sea with their ships, as had happened before on Easter. The cannon fire on the Poles was so heavy that they could not withdraw fast enough. Their cannonballs also traveled more than half again as far toward our camp as our balls did across the water, since the surrounding swamps were frozen and the balls could roll along on the ice so fast that one ball often took off the feet and legs of ten or twelve men, frequently both feet of the same man. During this blockade the Prussians frequently made attacks, although every time with great losses.

At the end of over four weeks the command came from General Vandamme,[1] or rather from Prince Jérôme, that both regiments from Württemberg should go by forced march to Silesia to the siege of Silberberg.

When we marched away, we had to get additional horses in the little town of Belgard to carry the knapsacks, etc. This brought me to misfortune, since my knapsack, cloak, bayonet, and the money which I had packed in a belt of my cloak, were lost. When I was in my quarters and learned this, I wanted a horse to ride to the other companies in order to look for my lost articles, but I had to make use of a military requisition and look for a horse with my landlord in the forest, since I saw that there was horse manure in the stable. When I had the horse but no saddle or bridle, I made a bridle out of a bit of rope and traveled about three miles in the surrounding villages but found nothing. At best I only got lost and did not know how to ask where I wanted to go; since because of the dialect there I could not remember the name of the village and I believed that I could depend on what I had remembered of the roads. Finally it grew dark, and with no other choice I had to let the horse go where it wished, and that proved the best choice. The horse walked half the night through heath and woods; and, since I did not let it graze from the ground, it went home to its village; and I had to be resigned to my loss.

From this village the march went through Pomerania and Poland to Breslau. From Kalisch on we obtained wagons and were all driven in them to the camp near Frankenstein and Reichenbach. We arrived there in the month of June.

Before the fortress of Silberberg, all the regiments from Württemberg and also Bavarian soldiers had laid siege. The stronghold could not be stormed because of its height and would not surrender. The ground plan of this fortress could be examined by many of our men who were captured, but only after the war. During the war they were not allowed even to see the way they had to go.

After two weeks had passed, a few regiments remained before this fortress; and the others, in which I belonged, had to begin the siege at Glatz. When the blockade of this stronghold was begun, the Württemberg troops took up their camp in a rye field just blooming, and the straw was of the right length to serve for the barracks, which was a great advantage in camping.

When I arrived in this field, I hastened to look for my brother, who was in the Lilienberg Regiment. Here we met, embraced, and greeted one another, and joy filled our hearts. Then he took me to his barracks and gave me trousers, shirts, and several other pieces of clothing which I needed, since, as I have already said, I had lost almost everything at Colberg.

Then, when the stronghold of Glatz was surrounded by blockade, several surprise attacks were undertaken against us, which always ended, nevertheless, in a loss to the Prussians. After two weeks had passed, we undertook against the town and the fortress an attack which started from each camp at about one o'clock at night. Everyone had to be careful to prevent any noise from the rifles and cannon, and we moved in columns through the grain fields toward the outposts. The men were already wet through up to their necks from the dew on the grain. Then the outposts began to fire, the command to storm was given, and everyone had to go through a river, at times up to his arms in water. A breastwork facing us was mounted, and under a rain of large and small bullets the Prussians along with their women and children were stabbed and shot to death, and some were hurled alive, together with their horses and cannon, over the sides of the walls. Then the Lilienberg Regiment pressed upon the city gates, an attempt which, in spite of great losses, was of no avail, however. While the enemy had to defend themselves around and in the crowded part of the city, a terrible shelling of light and heavy artillery broke in upon us, and all of us had to abandon the positions we had taken. Large mines were exploded in the breastwork, and everywhere there flew rockets, so-called pitch-rings, which could be put out only with small boxes as they fell on the ground.

So everyone returned to the camp in the "finest" disorder, and at daybreak everyone began looking up his friends. With fear-pressed heart I searched for my brother; and, as he was also looking for me, we found each other unharmed. Anyone who understands brotherly love can certainly imagine our joy at this moment.

When this attack was over, it was said that we would attack again the next night if the fortress did not surrender. This attack was not made, however, because of the announcement of peace. If anyone would or could be an onlooker at frightful explosions, he could get the finest view at a fortress attack, which is a more remarkable sight by far than a battle on a field. The bombs and grenades criss-crossing in the air in such great numbers, all floating like balls of fire in the air and exploding or bursting in the air or on the ground with a small cannon report, the slow ascent of each shell, the fast descent, often also a collision of them in the air—all this is a sight of moving beauty. It is different with the rockets which fly invisibly by with a small whisper. The grenades, however, and more so the bombs, behave like vultures in the air which race past the ear with storming wings.

We remained a few days longer in the camp, then came to a permanent camp in the region near Reichenbach, and were finally stationed every two weeks in another region. On St. Jacob's Day all the Württembergers had to leave Silesia, go by way of Frankfort-on-the-Oder, and take up permanent camp in the Brandenburg district, especially the region around Berlin near Stargard, Fürstenwalde, Beeskow, etc.

Here we stayed for eleven weeks among these poor peasants, who because of the infertility of the region had no provisions except potatoes, beans, and mutton. In speaking often of the good food which they had to give us, they hinted that they believed we must come from good country, since we, having the best of food, did not show any appreciation of it and because of our appetite had butchered all their sheep.

For one who wishes to discuss the poverty and its causes, my observations are set forth in the following manner: First, these people still owe their noblemen too much socage service in that the baron demands a quarter-share cottager's hired hand or son to work for him four, five, or six days weekly without wages. Likewise he takes a daughter for six years without paying her wages just as the reigning prince takes the son for his army. A half- or full-share cottager has to serve more, in proportion to the size of his property; so there are still villages where a man with his wife and children must work from three to five days for the nobleman, the fourth, fifth, or only the sixth day remaining for him to work for himself. However, he gets as much land from the baron for himself as he wants, or is able to till.

Second, the soil is only light sand, so that when sown to seed the tilled patches must even be beaten with a lath and, to prevent the blowing away of sand and seed, must be pressed down firmly. Naturally, therefore, only oats, potatoes (*"Undeln"*), and rye, seldom any wheat, can be grown.

Third, there is a lack of culture, especially of physical training, of willingness to work, of understanding and religion. Seldom does anyone go to church, only old grandmothers and old men, so that often, as I saw myself, the preacher would read his Sunday sermon for eight or ten persons with a similar lack of ardor. I learned also from my landlord, who had a boy of eleven or twelve years of age, that this boy could not read or write and did not know religious teachings. A book lying there gave me occasion to find this out.

As I was reading, I happened to run across the Ten Commandents. I asked whether the Ten Commandments were taught to the children in the schools. The landlord said, "Yes, they are supposed to be taught, but my son does not know them yet, nor can he read or write. I must demand, however, that he still be taught it." Since, therefore, these people are little educated even in their own religion, un-Christian and heretical books serve to make them hate other denominations, and such people are weak enough to believe fables of this kind. I became convinced of this as I read in such a book and afterward spoke of it to the landlord. Therefore I played the part of a gravedigger, bound a stone to this book, and sank it in the big lake.

After I had been in this village for three months, the entire corps journeyed home. The march went through Plauen, Nuremberg, Bayreuth, Ansbach, and Dinkelsbühl, into Ellwangen. The King awaited us and then reviewed us there on the Schlossfeld. It was extraordinarily cold on this day, although we did not consider this unusual, since we were already accustomed to cold. Before we came to Ellwangen, my company passed the night in the little town of Weiltingen, which is "Old Württembergian." There everyone was supposed to give shouts of joy at crossing the border, but this was followed by a good deal of swearing because of the bad quarters we were given there. This campaign was now ended, and my two sisters and friends visited us two brothers. The reunion was a joy which could not have been greater evidence of family love.

Campaign

of

1809

WHILE I WAS WORKING in various ways at my trade after the Prussian campaign, the war with Austria broke out in 1809, and I was called into the garrison at Stuttgart. My regiment and several others were already on the march to Schorndorf, and the route was to lead through Bavaria. On the way, however, a courier overtook us, bringing the command to march back to Stuttgart again the next day, and then we struck a route toward Tyrol through the Adlerberg territory. We came then through Hechingen, through the Killerthal, Saulgau, Altshausen, and then the Monastery of Weingarten. There we were already meeting outposts of the enemy, but we still had good quarters and especially a lot of wine from the Lake [of Constance].

When the Tyrolean insurgents heard of a large army reenforced by the allied Baden and French forces, they retreated, and we moved forward on all sides. The army then went through Ravensburg and to Hofen on the Lake of Constance while the enemy moved with several skirmishes to Lindau and finally back into the mountains.

In Hofen the Lilienberg Regiment was also stationed, in which my brother served, and we met in his quarters. It is easy to imagine that we two brothers rejoiced heartily at our reunion. The worry of one of us about the possible misfortune of the other was so much greater because we could seldom see and never protect each other.

After the aforesaid reunion I had to go through Buchhorn to Lindau. This latter city lies on an island in the lake, and a wooden bridge leads into it. The insurgents had to move out of this city for fear of being shut in. The first battalion of my regiment stayed ten weeks in this city, in which French horsemen were also stationed. During this time we had to make frequent attacks upon the enemy, among which the following were especially noteworthy.

As I stood at my outpost with the picket near the bleaching meadow facing Bregenz, the enemy moved in over the vineyards. The outposts had to move back to the picket. The picket fired, but the enemy approached. While each soldier fired wherever he could take a position, everyone stationed himself behind the bleaching house and took up the defense. To be able to aim better, I ran into a bleaching hut built of boards which lay well forward. A staircase went up from the outside, and I stationed myself on this, resting my rifle on the railing, where I could take aim at every man who approached. During the time while I was firing forty out of my sixty cartridges, the bullets kept raining down like hail upon my hut, and the enemy came too close upon me. Now I sprang down the steps and across the meadows back to the picket, which, however, was already retreating toward the city. Then I had to jump through gardens and hedges, and the enemy came to the gate just a little later than I did. I almost choked, gasping for breath.

When all of us had retreated into the city, the enemy remained outside the city three days, firing continually. We, however, had erected a bridge-head (breastwork) of sandbags and a trench and defensive iron spikes. We fired through the loopholes and from the wall with cannon and small guns. During the heavy shelling I shot a man in front of a garden house as he came a little way forward toward the breastwork and aimed into the loophole; but, after I shot and he suddenly fell, several others wanted to carry off this dead man, as was often done; however, the more openly it was done, the more often other men were hit too. Finally we fired with cannon, throwing projectiles into the large and beautiful garden houses, setting them all in flames. On the third day the enemy could no longer hold out, because of the heavy artillery fire, and moved back into the mountains.

As soon as the road was cleared, the trees standing in the gardens were cut down by the thousands, along with the beautiful box hedges which stood there tall and beautiful like walls, and the rest of the buildings were completely torn down, so that they would not be a hindrance to the shelling any more. This inflicted a damage of one million florins on the city.

After a time we again undertook a general attack, for which the Lilienberg Regiment, Baden and French soldiers, and the sharpshooters joined us. The enemy was attacked in front of Lindau and was driven in retreat back into the mountains. Before the attack volunteers were

called upon to advance by skirmishes, and I went with
them. The number was 160 men in all, and we were under
the command of a lieutenant. Under the continual firing
about fifty sharpshooters were cut off from us during the
pursuit and led captive into the mountains. All of us
volunteers pressed halfway up the mountain which was
two hours distant from Lindau in order to recover the
captives. When we saw that the columns advancing behind
us were no longer following but were dividing in the
middle and that our detachment had moved three quarters
of an hour too far away, we heard the firing far to the
left and far to the right as though it came from Kempten
and, to the right, from Bregenz. This seemed to be a
turning of our men into retreat, which assumption proved
to be true. Now the lieutenant wanted to retreat with us,
but we all complained at that and still wanted to bring
back the captives from the mountains. The lieutenant
would not give in, and we had to go back to a little village
at the foot of the mountains. When we came into this
village, we were fired upon from the houses and gardens
and our army had already retreated halfway toward Lindau. Everyone then had to rely upon his legs; and, amid
much firing, we had to run until we almost choked for
want of air. We met the whole corps in an oak wood a
half hour out of Lindau. Here we wanted to take a stand,
but could not because of the danger of being surrounded
by insurgents.

Now the detachment retreated slowly until near the
city, and then took up again the position for firing. Here
we held out for half an hour, everyone firing as much as
he could. The cannon were hauled out, but the grapeshot

fire did not help either, since the enemy formed a half-moon line and only a few could be hit, for they lay down on the ground behind the hedges, trees, and hills, while every shot of theirs could hit our compressed column. Finally too many of our men fell, and the enemy drew near the city gate in order to cut everyone off; this hurried our retreat into the city.

Noteworthy was the state of the peasants who had to drive the wagons to pick up the wounded and who had to come right along at the time of the attack. Four men and four horses were hitched to each wagon. As soon as the firing began, they had to stay with us. From then on, none of them could be seen sitting upright on his horse: they were all lying down on their horses, and those on the wagons flung themselves down amidst a fearful howling. In addition, they were given blows because of their fear.

3. NEAR EVE, 29 JUNE 1812. A. CUANTH, LITHOGRAPHER. A FORAGING PARTY ON THE MOVE.

During this time that I was at Lindau, the second battalion of the Franquemont Regiment, which was stationed at Wangen and Isny, was made completely captive. Later peace was made, and we marched into Bregenz, a town up on the Lake of Constance. However, the entrance into this city was looked upon as a somewhat hostile move. For the sake of security several regiments coming from the mountains entered it from behind, and those from Lindau moved in from the front.

Indeed, the Regiment of Lilienberg had once before been forced to flee after a conquest of the town. It happened in this way: while the soldiers were looking about for booty in the cellars and houses, the enemy moved into the town and drove everyone out through the narrow pass in the mountain, which has three outlets. On this occasion the enemy should have pressed their advantage. Rather than rushing dispersed into the attack, they might better have occupied the three outlets and made captives of everyone. Instead, they only fired down from the mountains at their fleeing enemies in the pass, not having occupied the outlets strongly enough.

When our before-mentioned entry into Bregenz began, there was once more disorder among the soldiery. Cellars were broken into, and wine was carried out in buckets everywhere. Even several kegs were left running. Everyone became intoxicated until finally a strict order put an end to all this. We drank especially a great deal of very thick red Tyrolean wine, and we had everything in abundance. When, however, a new day arrived and all had moved into their quarters, everything became quiet, and the property of the citizens was safeguarded.

I stayed there almost three weeks at the home of a chimney sweep, together with nine other men, and we had everything, in particular as much as we could drink, wine and cherry brandy. After three weeks my regiment was moved to Dornbirn, which was a large marketing center lying in the Rhine Valley between Switzerland and Tyrol. In this town I came into the house of a furrier, who himself was still with the insurgents. His wife had a little child about three-quarters of a year old. This child was remarkably beautiful, and I, too, had my fun with it.

Once I gave this child some brandy to drink. Little by little the child took a liking to it, so that it became a bit intoxicated and so gleeful that I had to keep it from falling down from the pillow; this was great fun and did not do the child any harm. I stayed another period of about three weeks in these quarters, and in the entire village the people were quite friendly.

The householders in this village and the surrounding region have several maids who come from the Tyrolean Alps. These maids are especially remarkable for their dress. All their black skirts are of one piece with the bodice and have a great number of pleats all around. Upon their heads they wear large black caps, which likewise have curious pleats and are large and round like beehives in form. These maids have especially pretty and rosy-colored faces, which is said to come from eating milk and cheese. As to sociability, however, there is not much to say for them, since they are shy and not very talkative. They showed this even more toward orderly soldiers, as I know from experience, since there were two such maids in my house. It often happened, when they were sitting at their meal and I would joke with them decently, that they would jump up from the table and run out of the room, and then it was difficult to get them to come back again.

Regarding the fertility of this region, there is not much rye or German wheat, so much the more corn, however. The bread in particular is usually of nothing but corn. When you look at the bread, you believe that it is made of the finest kernels. When eating it, however, you notice it is coarse, heavy, and soggy. Wood is not cheap either; and in place of it in the entire Rhine Valley they dig peat, that is, sod which is a grayish red. This is cut and piled up, dried in the air and sun, and then burned in stoves instead of wood.

4. *A BIVOUAC NEAR MALIATHUI, 5 JULY 1812. PRINTED BY G. KÜSTNER. SOLDIERS TRADING FOR FURS WITH LOCAL JEWISH MERCHANTS.*

During this time, from spring to fall, we always had the great snow-capped mountains before, and later around us. Every time that it had rained, even in the greatest heat in August, one could see that the mountains were covered with new snow to a third of the distance down from the top.

In the month of October, we again marched homeward, and the route led through Wangen, Ravensburg, Altdorf, and Waldsee, and from there to Biberach, where we all had to stay for some time, being quartered in the surrounding villages. I also was assigned to a village and to the house of a well-to-do peasant who had a sister, a nun who was living at home. Since I would read books frequently on certain days and the nun noticed my behavior, she asked me why I always read and was so thoughtful. I said that my former circumstances gave me occasion to do that.

Since I kept trying to be pleasant to her and was able to draw her attention more and more toward me, she asked others about my situation. Now I thought that since this thing had been started it must be carried on. I spoke to all my comrades located in the village, saying that they should call me at times "Miller," at other times "Walter," and again "Kapuziner." This was done. Then the nun said to me, "Now I know, indeed, where your devout reading comes from. You may as well confess it to me." So then I did her the favor and told her that my brother had been a priest and I a Capuchin monk, that I had already vowed my chastity, and also that my name had been Miller instead of Walter, which the malicious soldiers always applied to me. I finally told her that she had evidence here in my beard which I still wore on my chin.

From now on, these pious hosts were very sympathetic toward me, and the nun told me her entire cloister story, and they had a liking for me above all other soldiers, so much so that the old father wept tears. Especially when I left, he wept with the others, begging that if I loved them I should inform them of my future fate in distant places. They even wanted to accompany me for several hours.

After the years 1810 and 1811 had passed by and I was, in 1811, at the house of my godfather, Master Craftsman Häfele, the innkeeper at Ellwangen, war once more broke out.

Campaign

of

1812 and 1813

IN THE MONTH OF JAN-
uary, 1812, I was recalled to the
garrison of Schorndorf. From here
the line of march went through
Calw, Wüstenroth, and Oehringen.
In the villages about Oehringen the
regiments remained four or five
days until the inspection was com-
pleted in Oehringen. From here the entire corps marched
through Künzelsau, Mergentheim, Weikersheim, and
through the Würzburg district, where it was generally
rumored that we were going to Spain and would embark
on the Baltic Sea. Although the outlook did not seem
good, I and all the soldiers were very merry, always singing
and dancing, especially since throughout the entire Würzburg country the quarters and eating and drinking were
very good, particularly because of the large supply of
wine, so that everyone had his field flask voluntarily filled
with wine and his pockets with cookies at the time of
departure. Moreover, the beautiful villages on the Main
River, surrounded by vineyards, fruit trees, and grain
fields, put everyone in a happy mood.

About the middle of March, the army continued on
its way through Saxe-Coburg, where a wooded and mountainous region began; the pine trees were especially plen-
tiful. In these mountains we came upon a valley which

led out of the Thuringian Forest. In this valley there were sawmills every two or three hundred paces, and between them were little hamlets. When the valley turned to the right and our march to the left, as it went through the Thuringian Forest itself to Saxe-Weimar, we had to climb high as if up a roof. In this huge forest, snow still lay two feet deep, though during the whole march no more was to be seen. In the middle of the forest was a game park which was tightly enclosed with planks to a height of twelve feet and which was about an hour's walk long. The city where we afterward spent the night lay about an hour's walk away in the valley. From Weimar we turned somewhat to the left, continued through a few cities toward Leipsic, and in April entered Leipsic.

In the city of Leipsic anyone could see what was going to happen, since as many "Frenchies" as could slip through came crowding through the gates. Leipsic was packed with soldiers, and I was in quarters with 150 men; yet the landlord to whom we were assigned put us all in one building, the former theater building, which was a hall 100 feet long and 60 feet wide. Triple rows of tables stood ready in the hall, very beautifully set and loaded with beer, brandy, butter, cheese, and white bread. After all had sat down, everybody ate and drank while eight servants brought in the warm meal, which consisted of white soup, two kinds of meat, and several kinds of vegetables. In addition, something cold was served for dessert, and drinks were served in abundance throughout the whole afternoon. We stayed here two days until the line of march formed by columns and the departure was ordered.

After leaving Leipsic, we found the quarters somewhat worse on account of the huge army of soldiers, and the march turned toward Torgau. I had been in Torgau in 1807. In the meantime the city had built new fortifications. About the city, which it took an hour to walk around, there had been added two moats and besides four buttressed walls of nothing but beautifully hewn stones which had been shipped down the Elbe from Bohemia. These new huge walls especially attracted my attention, since I could examine them as a mason and a stonecutter; and so I saw that each of them was ten feet thick and that buttresses were set into the ground every ten feet behind them, each of them in turn ten feet thick and ten feet long. I noticed especially the beautiful jointing of the stones, most of which were ten feet long and three feet square and had been laid over the wall lengthwise. On

5. BETWEEN KIRGALICZKY AND SOUDERVA, 30 JUNE 1812. DAVID & VANDERBUCK, LITHOGRAPHERS. SOLDIERS FORDING A RIVER.

the other side of the Elbe there were also casements facing eastward, which were all, even the roofwork, built of beautifully hewn stone.

And then we went farther and came to Fürstenwalde, a middle-sized city in the Brandenburg district. It was the region where my regiment had lain in fixed quarters for eleven weeks in 1807, and so many of us went to see our former landlords; several women also found their once beloved soldiers, although several men were hiding for good reason and did not wish to be found for fear they would be called a father. In this city I was quartered with a beer brewer. We stayed there several days. The opportunity was also taken to invite soldiers to communion, for which four Catholic and four Lutheran clergymen had been sent along with the corps from home. The church was Lutheran, but we held the Catholic services there, too; so I received communion. We were still very lively in this town, singing and living cheerfully, although we could imagine the unusual campaign before us; but everyone always believes in, and hopes for, the best. I also looked after my saber and made it very sharp at a turner's and tempered it in fire so that it would not break off. I saw in the eastern suburb of this little town a house, the timber framing of which was filled with bones cross-wise; instead of being walled in, these bones had moss between them. In general, the types of buildings in this region are of a poor appearance and quality so that a like condition may be assumed about the farming. From there the line of march turned toward Frankfort-on-the-Oder, where a halt was made. Here we were quartered for three days, and by this time we had to be contented with poor food and army bread. We had to drill even on Ascension Day; so General Hügel tried to remind his royal highness, the Crown Prince, not to drill, saying that it was a holiday. The Crown Prince, however, gave this answer: "I will do you a favor, General, and not arrest you. Do you think I don't know what day it is?" This indignant mood of our Crown Prince might well have been caused by the transfer of the Württemberg corps to General Ney, since the day before Ney had attached us to his 25th division and the 3rd army corps; and our Crown Prince, feeling his honor injured, was, therefore, angry with us.

From Frankfort the march was continued to Poland through the village of Reppen, where the use of the German language stopped, and the manners and culture made a strange impression. It was the month of May, and the air swarmed with May bugs so amazingly that it was hard to keep your eyes open in the evening. The bugs were so very thick that they darkened the atmosphere, and everyone was busy shaking them out of his face and hair. Here it became necessary for each person to seek and cook his own provisions, although requisitioning was forbidden. However, everyone still had his full strength, and courage was still alive in every soldier. But from day to day privation and hunger increased, and it became necessary for the regiment to requisition and slaughter livestock so that the men could have some meat in addition to the potatoes and grits which they found here and there. Bread was rare, and there was nothing at hand to buy.

Now we came to a Polish government town, Posen, to which I had brought the horses, wagons, and servants of a Polish general, as I noted in connection with the campaign of 1807. From there we went to Gnesen, also an important city, where I, likewise in 1807, had announced in eight villages that food must be delivered for Napoleon and where I had had to spend almost two weeks. In these towns it was still possible to buy provisions here and there, and supposedly quarters were still available there. The march continued through [Inowr]azlav, also a city where I had been during the Prussian campaigns, and all the roads of this district were still well known to me.

On Corpus Christi Day we marched into the city of Thorn, which lies on the northern bank of the Vistula River, another city in which I had been during the year of 1807. Here for the first time we saw all the corps streaming together. All the gates were jammed, and the regiments had to wind through the streets in a great throng. We still obtained quarters. However, we had to prepare our own food from our rationed meat and bread. The meat came from the salted ice pits; there was a rumor that it had been stored from the war of 1807— the condition of the meat made the rumor seem credible, since the meat appeared bluish-black and was salty as herrings. It was already tender enough to eat, and we boiled it a few times only to draw off the muriatic acid; and then the broth, not being useful for soup, had to be thrown out.

Since we stayed in Thorn on Corpus Christi Day, I attended the service in the great City Church, where I heard what was to me a very unusual sermon, because it was given in Polish and I could not understand anything of it. I also climbed the high, broad tower, which had more than a hundred steps, and saw the eight bells. The largest bell had a clapper that was taller than I was. An equally large clapper leaned against the wall, and I could not pull it by its upper part from the wall. This city had been improved as a fortress since my visit in 1807. The near-by heights were dug away, and ramparts were built, although with only wooden beams filled in between with sand instead of massive walls.

Now the orders led us from Thorn to Mariampol. The march there went through Seeburg, Bischofstein, and Lagarben. The roads were sandy, and dust covered our clothing. Thence we went to a village called Löventin, where we saw a strange sight: we could count as many as thirty stork nests; almost all the storks had nested in tall willow trees and stalked around the swamps in flocks like the geese at home. The route led us on through Nordenburg and Darkehmen. Then we came to a little town known as Kalvaria, which lay on a dead-level in a barren region. Here only a noon halt was made, and no one had anything to eat. Since all is allowed to necessity, this little town, although already plundered, could not remain unsearched. All the soldiers ran for food and water, and it so happened that what provisions the inhabitants had hidden were found and brought into the camp, even though it was Polish country and, therefore, friendly. Because of this fact, the inhabitants of the town complained to our Crown Prince; and, therefore, the command came that the first soldier who thus left camp would be shot. I returned to the camp, however, just in time. The determination of our Crown Prince had risen so high that he rode along the front with a pistol and held it on the breasts of some soldiers so that one might have almost believed some of them were going to be shot, but their dire need with nothing to eat may have stopped him.

Daily the hardships increased, and there was no hope of bread. My colonel spoke to us once and said that we could hope for no more bread until we crossed the enemy border. The most anyone might still get was a little lean beef, and hunger made it necessary to dig up the fields for the potatoes already sprouting, which were, however, very sweet and almost inedible. One also heard everywhere that several men had already shot themselves

6. *A BIVOUAC NEAR KOKUTISCZKI (KUKUTISHKI), 9 JULY 1812. SOL-DIERS EVICT A JEW FROM CAMP, WHILE OTHERS LAUGHINGLY LOOK ON. IN THE DISTANCE, CHRISTIAN WORSHIPPERS VENERATE THE CROSS BEFORE A SMALL WOODEN CHURCH.*

because of hardship: in particular, an officer had cut his throat on that very same day. Finally we came to the Memel River, where the Russian border was. The town of Poniemon was located there. Everyone rejoiced to see the Russian boundary at last. We encamped at the foot of the hill this side of the river, and everyone thought that he should make his knapsack as light as possible. I, too, searched through my pieces of clothing and threw away vests, unnecessary cleaning articles, trousers, etc. Here we had to make a halt until the pontoons were brought up and several bridges were constructed across the water. Now we believed that the Russians would wait on the other bank and attack, but nothing happened. Bonaparte fired upon the high points held by the Russians with a few cannon and sent his cavalry across the water. The Russians, however, withdrew after a short encounter.

On June 25 the army went over the bridges. We now believed that, once in Russia, we need do nothing but forage—which, however, proved to be an illusion. The town of Poniemon was already stripped before we could enter, and so were all the villages. Here and there a hog ran around and then was beaten with clubs, chopped with sabers, and stabbed with bayonets; and, often still living, it would be cut and torn to pieces. Several times I succeeded in cutting off something; but I had to chew it and eat it uncooked, since my hunger could not wait for a chance to boil the meat. The worst torture was the march, because the closed ranks forced all to go in columns; the heat and the dust flared up into our eyes as if from smoking coal heaps. The hardship was doubled by the continual halting of the troops whenever we came to a swamp or a narrow road. Often one had to stand for half an hour; then another such period was spent catching up and drudging away without water or food.

The march proceeded day and night toward Vilkomirz and Eve. Meanwhile it rained ceaselessly for several days, and the rain was cold. It was all the more disagreeable because nothing could be dried. Bodily warmth was our only salvation from freezing to death. I had on only one pair of blue linen trousers, which I had bought at Thorn, since I had thrown away my underwear because of the former heat. Thus I was constantly wet for two days and two nights, so that not a spot on my body was dry. Nevertheless, I did not remain behind, although I could not see the way at night and slid in every direction on account of the clay soil. Indeed, the soldiers fell about me so incessantly that most of them were completely covered with mud and some were left lying behind.

During the third night a halt was made in a field which was trampled into a swamp. Here we were ordered to camp and to make fires, since neither village nor forest could be seen and the rain continued without end. You can imagine in what a half-numbed condition everyone stood here. What could we do? There was nothing that we could do but stack the rifles in pyramids and keep moving in order not to freeze. Finally an estate was found off to one side, and all the soldiers by groups immediately ran to build a shelter. There was nothing else to do except to use all our strength and to pull out poles and straw; so I with assistance built a little shelter, but my strength did not last long enough to collect firewood. I lay in the tent shelter, hungry and wet. The comrades, however, who came in and lay down upon me served as a warm cover.

When dawn came, I hurried again to the manor. Meanwhile a cellar full of brandy had been discovered. I, too, pushed myself into the cellar and filled my field flask. I returned to the shelter with this and drank it without even any bread. Then by noon I noticed that half the men had stayed back and several had suffocated in the swamp. The brandy helped, but many a man drank himself to death because he would become numbed and would freeze on account of the wet and cold. My drummer, by the name of Schäfer, met such an end.

In the evening, when some cow's meat was distributed, with difficulty we started a fire, so that meat and broth soon warmed our stomachs. Then the march continued toward the little town of Maliaty, where a two-day halt was made and the sick were taken to the hospital. In this bivouac we obtained some meat; but most of the men could no longer digest the pure meat, diarrhea seized many, and they had to be abandoned. In this camp I took the opportunity to wash my shirt and trousers. It happened to be good weather; but, in order to obtain water for drinking and cooking, holes were dug into the swamps three feet deep in which the water collected. The water was very warm, however, and was reddish-brown with millions of little red worms so that it had to be bound in linen and sucked through with the mouth. This was, of course, a hard necessity on our nature and ways.

Then we had to march farther through the villages of Kosatschisna [?], Labonary, Diescony [?], Drysviaty,

Braslav, toward Disna, where we arrived in the middle of July. The men were growing weaker and weaker every day and the companies smaller and smaller. The march was kept up day and night. One man after another stretched himself half-dead upon the ground; most of them died a few hours later; several, however, suddenly fell to the ground dead. The chief cause of this was thirst, for in most districts there was no water fit for drinking, so that the men had to drink out of ditches in which were lying dead horses and dead men. I often marched away from the columns for several hours in search of water, but seldom could I return with any water and had to go thirsty. All the towns not only were completely stripped but were also half-burned.

Finally we arrived at Polotsk, a large city on the other side of the Dvina River. In this region I once left the bivouac to seek provisions. There were eight of us, and we came to a very distant village. Here we searched all the houses. There were no peasants left. I later realized how heedless I had been, since each one ran into a house alone, broke open everything that was covered, and searched all the floors and still nothing was found. Finally, when we assembled and were ready to leave, I once more inspected a little hut somewhat removed from the village. Around it from top to bottom were heaped bundles of hemp and shives, which I tore down; and, as I worked my way to the ground, sacks full of flour appeared. Now I joyfully called all my comrades so that we might dispose of the booty. In the village we saw sieves; these we took to sift the flour mixed with chaff an inch long; and, after that, we refilled the sacks.

Then the question of carrying and dividing the grain arose, but it occurred to me that I had seen a horse in one of the houses. Everyone immediately hurried to find the horse. We found two instead of one, but unfortunately they were both colts, and one could not be used at all. We took the largest, placed two sacks on it, and started out very slowly. While we were marching there, the Russians saw us from a distance with this booty; and at the same moment we saw a troop of peasants in the valley, about fifty. These ran toward us. What could we do but shoot at them? I, however, led the horse, and a second man held the sacks while the rest fired, one after another, so that the peasants divided in order not to be hit so easily; but they could not take the sacks away from us.

7. *A BIVOUAC OF 31 AUGUST 1812. G. KÜSTNER, PRINTER. EMMINGER AND BAUMEISTER, LITHOGRAPHERS. NAPOLEON'S TROOPS CUTTING HAY FOR CAVALRY HORSES, WITH A GREAT MANOR HOUSE IN THE BACKGROUND.*

We hurried toward the bivouac, but on the way we found a deep stream of water, and only a round tree trunk lay across it. Now the question arose how to take the horse and sacks across. I said, "Why, I will carry the sacks across, and we will throw the horse into the water," and, indeed, I succeeded in getting over the narrow bridge in an upright position without the use of handrails, which feat might have cost me my life, since the river was very deep. Then the horse was thrown in and driven across with stones, the sacks were then reloaded, and we finally marched into bivouac. That was a joy! Whatever each person could not use was distributed. Then dough was made, and little balls were molded with the hands and baked, or rather roasted, in the fire. This food lasted me a week, and I thanked God for the chance gift which had remained buried under the shives until I came.

We then marched farther in a somewhat more eastern direction through Ula, Beshenkovichi, and Ostrovno, and near the end of July toward Vitebsk. Often on the way to Vitebsk we undertook a raiding excursion. Some thirty of our men went off the main route to find a still inhabited and unstripped village. We collected our strength and walked from three to four hours in hopes of rejoining the army at the second bivouac.

We were fortunate and found a village where everything still seemed to be in order. To safeguard our small group, we left a rear-guard behind and agreed that they should report with certain shooting signals a possible attack from the Russians. As we entered the village, a man at once approached us who was probably sent as an interpreter from the mayor to learn our desires. We told him that we required provisions for the army—if we received them voluntarily, force would not be used. He reported it to the village, but the answer was of no good; so we were compelled two by two to take a house and search it. I joined forces with a comrade but found nothing except milk and cabbage ("*Kapuke*"[2]).

A wooden hut stood on a farm. This was locked, and the peasants would not open it. When we broke down the door, a woman who was with child came running at us as if mad and wanted to throw us out, but we forced her back with gentle thrusts. Here we obtained some flour, eggs, and fat. When all brought their findings together later, our booty was considerable. I am telling of this undertaking to show the ways of the Russian subjects. If they had voluntarily removed the simple covers [of their storage places], much of the household furniture would have remained unspoiled, for it was necessary to raise the floors and the beams in order to find anything and to turn upside down everything that was covered. Under one such floor, which had large beams resting side by side, we found pots full of sausages stuffed into casings four to five feet long and filled with pieces of bacon and meat an inch thick. Although such sausages already had a fierce smell, they were quickly eaten. Here were also hidden pots filled with lumps of cheese, which according to the customs of the country had been placed as milk on the fire and had been allowed to curdle so that the milk, cheese, and fat floated about in chunks. The cheese and fat were still left for us.

In another well-plundered village nothing could be found in the houses; and so, urged on by our hunger, we dug in the ground. Here I with several others removed a large pile of wood which had probably just been put there. We removed this, dug into the ground, and found a covered roof of planks. There was an opening under this from ten to twelve feet deep. Inside there were honey jars and wheat covered with straw. When we had all this, we opened the jars and saw a solid, white substance with the appearance of hard wax. It was so hard that one had trouble breaking off a piece with his saber; but, as soon as it was put on the fire, it all melted to very clear honey. Now I had honey to eat for a week, although without bread. I ate the wheat raw and wild calamus from the swamps; and, in general, what garden roots were to be found had to serve the most extreme hunger.

After this raiding excursion we again met the corps in bivouac; and we came then, on August 16, toward the city of Smolensk. Here my company had only 25 fit men. At Vitebsk already regiments had been formed into a few battalions, and many officers were left without duties; among them was my captain, whose name was Arrant. Here everyone had to be prepared for battle. The city lay before us on a long ascending height, and on the other side was the Dnieper River. Even on the night of our arrival there were a few skirmishes with the outposts and vanguard.

On the morning of August 17, every regiment was set in motion, and all advanced in columns against the Russians. Here every regiment without exception was under fire. Again and again the troops attempted assaults, but because of the greater number of the Russians we were forced back every time on this day, since their heavy artillery stood on the heights and could hit everything. Finally by night we had made good our position on the heights overlooking the city, and the battle was discontinued. In the course of these events hunger could no longer be thought of. During the night, however, I ate from my little bit of honey and raw supplies without being able to cook. The thought of the coming day alternated with fitful sleep, and in fantasy the many dead men and horses came as a world of spirits before the last judgment. Since I did not suffer the misfortune of being wounded, I thought: "God, Thou hast allowed me to live till now. I thank Thee and offer up my sufferings to Thee and pray Thee at the same time to take me further into Thy protection."

This and several other pious meditations I had with

8. *NEAR KOKUSCZKINA, 11 JULY 1812. H. KURTZ, PRINTER. BAU-MEISTER, LITHOGRAPHER. A FORAGING PARTY, LADEN WITH PIL-FERED LIVESTOCK. THE MILEPOST INDICATES 71[?] VERSTS TO MOSCOW.*

God, and I considered my destiny. Although it was never quiet the entire night and though a new battle might have started at any hour, none of all my miseries was so hard and depressing as the thought of my brothers, sisters, and friends. This thought was my greatest pain, which I sought to repress with this hope: "With God everything is possible; so I will depend upon His further help."

As soon as the day broke—here I cannot omit the description of the length of the day and the shortness of the night. Many times when we went into bivouac for the night, the great glow of the sun was still in the sky so that there was only a brief interval between the setting and the rising sun. The redness remained very bright until sunrise. On waking one believed that it was just getting dark, but instead it became bright daylight. The nighttime lasted three hours at most, with the glow of the sun continuing. So, as soon as the day broke—we marched against the city. The river was crossed below the city. The suburbs on the northern side were stormed, set on fire, and burned up. My company's doctor, named Stäuble, had his arm shot away in crossing the stream, and he died afterward. No longer could I pay any attention to my comrades and, therefore, knew not in what way they perished or were lost. Everyone fired and struck at the enemy in wild madness, and no one could tell whether he was in front, in the middle, or behind the center of the army.

Finally, while cannon balls kept on raining out of the city, we stormed it. With the help of heavy cannon, most of the supporting piers on the high old city wall, on which the Russians were defending themselves from the inside, were partially destroyed. We broke through the gates, pressed from all sides against the city, and put the enemy to flight. When I entered the city, we went toward the cloisters and churches. I also hurried into the great church which stood to the right in the city on a hill facing the valley. I did not meet any of the enemy within, however. Only priests (*"Bopen"*[3]) were there praying. They had on long black cowls, ragged hose, and old slippers. The church was large and on the inside built round. It had many holy images and altars as ours do. The only difference was that there was no holy water. The church had five towers, one on each corner and one in the middle of the roof. On every tower were triple iron crosses, and from each cross went intervening chains from one tower to another; this created a beautiful appearance from without.

After the Russians had been stormed from the two suburbs, from which one road on the left leads to St. Petersburg and another on the right to Moscow, and after the wooden houses there lay in ruins, we resorted in the evening to the former camping ground. Here one saw the wounded men brought together to be operated on in a brick kiln which lay on the heights above the city. Many arms and legs were amputated and bandaged. It all looked just like a slaughter house. In the city itself over half of the buildings were burned; these included, especially in the upper part of the city, many large, massive houses which were burned out on the inside. Many roofs of sheet copper were rolled up and lay about. In one building west of the city I saw the lower story filled with paper, and on top it was burned black; probably all the official documents had been hurried to that place.

On August 19, the entire army moved forward, and pursued the Russians with all speed. Four or five hours' farther up the river another battle started, but the enemy did not hold out long, and the march now led to Moshaisk, the so-called "Holy Valley." From Smolensk to Moshaisk the war displayed its horrible work of destruction: all the roads, fields, and woods lay as though sown with people, horses, wagons, burned villages and cities; everything looked like the complete ruin of all that lived. In particular, we saw ten dead Russians to one of our men, although every day our numbers fell off considerably. In order to pass through woods, swamps, and narrow trails, trees which formed barriers in the woods had to be removed,

9. A BIVOUAC NEAR LIOZNA (LIASMA), 4 AUGUST 1812. G. KÜSTNER, PRINTER. EMMINGER, LITHOGRAPHER. ANOTHER FRUITFUL FORAGING EXPEDITION.

and wagon barricades of the enemy had to be cleared away. In such numbers were the Russians lying around that it seemed as if they were all dead. The cities in the meantime were Dorogobush, Semlevo, Viasma, and Gshatsk. The march up to there, as far as it was a march, is indescribable and inconceivable for people who have not seen anything of it. The very great heat, the dust which was like a thick fog, the closed line of march in columns, and the putrid water from holes filled with dead people, and cattle brought everyone close to death; and eye pains, fatigue, thirst, and hunger tormented everybody. God! how often I remembered the bread and beer which I had enjoyed at home with such an indifferent pleasure! Now, however, I must struggle, half wild, with the dead and living. How gladly would I renounce for my whole life the warm food so common at home if I only did not lack good bread and beer now! I would not wish for more all my life. But these were empty, helpless thoughts. Yes, the thought of my brothers and sisters so far away added to my pain! Wherever I looked, I saw the soldiers with dead, half-desperate faces. Many cried out in despair, "If only my mother had not borne me!" Some demoralized men even cursed their parents and their birth.

These voices, however, raised my soul to God, and I often spoke in quietude, "God, Thou canst save me; but, if it is not Thy will, I hope that my sins will be forgiven because of my sufferings and pains and that my soul will ascend to Thee." With such thoughts I went on trustingly to meet my fate.

On September 7, every corps was assigned its place,

and the signal to attack was given.[4] Like thunderbolts the
firing began both against and from the enemy. The earth
was trembling because of the cannon fire, and the rain
of cannon balls crossed confusedly. Several entrenchments
were stormed and taken with terrible sacrifices, but the
enemy did not move from their place. The French Guard,[5]
according to order, was placed behind the attacking corps
to bring about the final decision. Now the two armies
moved more vigorously against one another, and the death
cries and shattering gunfire seemed a hell. Nine entrenchments were stormed, the French threatened to sur-
round the enemy from the front, and finally the enemy
gave way.

This beautiful grain region without woods and villages could now be compared to a cleared forest, a few
trunks here and there looking gray and white [?]. Within
a space an hour and a half long and wide, the ground
was covered with people and animals. There were groans
and whines on all sides. The stream separated the battlefield into two parts. On the left of the water stood a
row of a few houses which looked as if transformed into
a chapel for the dead. Over the river there was a wooden
bridge that had been burned. On account of the conges-
tion before and during the burning, the banks on both
sides of the bridge were filled with dead piled three and
four deep. Particularly the wounded who could still move
hurried to the river to quench their thirst or to wash their
wounds; but the suffering brothers had no help, no hope
of rescue: hunger, thirst, and fire were their death.

Although this terrible sight looked like a kingdom
of the dead, the people had, nevertheless, become so

indifferent to their feelings that they all ran numbly like shades of death away from the piteous crying. We moved forward and camped by a forest on a height facing Moscow; it was a wood of green trees. Here we not only had nothing to eat but also no water to drink, because of the high camp site; and the road through the fields was still covered with dead Russians. Now we traveled with somewhat higher hopes toward Moscow yet with the expectation that we should clash again with the Russians, but the Russians thought themselves too weak and went through the city setting fire to many parts, and the inhabitants were abandoned. Our troops came unexpectedly, something which the Russians before had believed impossible, because there never had been a foreign enemy who had reached and conquered the old city of the Tsar, the capital city. All the merchants and people of the city

10. BATTLE NEAR SMOLENSK, 5 AUGUST 1812. PHOTOENGRAVED BY I. GOFFERT FROM A PAINTING BY P. VON HESS.

could not flee swiftly enough to save themselves, and many costly articles were left behind. Even though the French Guard occupied the city first and took possession of wine, bread, etc., for their army, there still remained a good deal for us, the allies. We marched in, too, and took quarters behind the Kremlin in the so-called German suburb, which ran from west to east behind the city proper.

On the march into the city or rather on the march toward it, from a hill in a forest an hour and a half away, we saw the huge city lying before us. Clouds of fire, red smoke, great gilded crosses of the church towers glittered, shimmered, and billowed up toward us from the city. This holy city was like the description of the city of Jerusalem, over which our Saviour wept; it even resembled the horror and the wasting according to the Gospel. Farther inward toward the city was a wide plain; and in front of the city ran the stream Alia,[6] over which there was a wooden bridge. As we marched through, I observed as much as I could: there were broad streets, long straight alleys, tall buildings massively built of brick, church towers with burned roofs and half-melted bells, and copper roofs which had rolled from the buildings; everything was un-inhabited and uninhabitable. After a few hours' walking we went past the palace (Kremlin). Here was the stream Kremlin[7] in an open, walled canal which runs through the city. At the lower end of the palace a street led toward the right to a beautiful parade ground; and behind this was the German suburb, which the Württemberg corps occupied for three weeks.

Here one could find and buy provisions; for each soldier was now citizen, merchant, innkeeper, and baker of Moscow. Everyone tried to dress as much as possible with silks and materials of all colors. Only tailors were lacking; silks, muslins, and red Morocco leather were all abundant. Things to eat were not wanting either. Whoever could find nothing could buy something and vegetables in sufficient quantity stood in the fields. Particularly was there an abundance of beets, which were as round and large as bowling balls and fiery red throughout. There were masses of cabbage three and four times as large in size as cabbage heads that we would consider large. The district called Muscovy is more favored in agriculture and climate, and more civilized than the regions toward St. Petersburg and those through which we had come. It was still good weather, and one could sleep warm enough under a coat at night.

After we had been citizens of Moscow for four weeks, we lost our burgher rights again. Napoleon refused the peace treaty proposed to him,[8] and the army which had advanced some thirty hours' farther on had to retreat, because the Russian army stationed in Moldavia was approaching. Now it was October 17, and Napoleon held an army review and announced the departure for October 18, early in the morning at 3 o'clock, with the warning that whoever should delay one hour would fall into the hands of the enemies. All beer, brandy, etc., was abandoned and whatever was still intact was ordered to be burned. Napoleon himself had the Kremlin undermined and blown up.[9] The morning came, and each took his privilege of citizenship [Bürgerrecht] upon his shoulders and covered it with his coat cape of strong woolen cloth, and everybody had bread pouches of red Morocco leather

11. "THIS FIRE WILL ILLUMINE FOR GENERATIONS THE FEROCITY OF NAPOLEON AND THE GLORY OF RUSSIA." CAPTIONED WITH A QUOTE FROM A RESCRIPT (1812) FROM THE EMPEROR TO COUNT ROSTOPCHIN, THIS WOODCUT SHOWS THE GATES AND TOWERS OF THE KREMLIN RINGED WITH FLAME AND BILLOWING SMOKE.

at his side, all had an odd appearance as they set out; they filled, as far as it was possible, everything with sugar and the so-called Moscow tea in order to withstand the future misery. The sugar melted out of the merchant shops in the conflagration and, half-burnt, resembled a brownish gray glauber salt.[10]

When we assembled in the morning, my company was 25 privates strong, and all companies were more or less of this size. The march went forth to the right from behind the eastern side of the city, and we moved past the city on the south. There were two bridges thrown across the river below us, and the smoke from the flames surged up behind us. Up on the heights past the bridge to the left of the road stood a cloister in which there was a flour storeroom where everyone fetched as much as he could carry. Beyond the bridge there was a cabbage patch where millions of cabbage heads were still standing: it pained me not to be able to take along even one of these heads, since I fully expected the utmost famine.

From Moscow the road led south through Malo Jaroslavetz toward Kaluga. Near Jaroslavetz in the evening the Russian Moldavian army, which had come from Turkey, met us. In this city I was ordered on guard at the headquarters of the general staff while the army encamped in front of the city. Here the inhumanity of the commanders began to mount: the remaining troops' weapons were inspected, and many who did not have their weapons fairly rust-free got 12 to 20 strokes with a club until they were near desperation. While I looked after my post, a comrade said to me that he had on a near-by wagon a little cask of wine brought along from Moscow and that since everything would be destroyed that day anyhow we would drink it up. We drank and also let others drink from it, but all of us said, "How will this turn out?"

In the morning Major von Schaumberg saw me and noticed that I was still alert and spirited. He addressed me, saying that I ought to stay with him and take care of him along with his attendant. I consented and took over a horse and his equipage. Then everyone packed up, and the enemy attacked us. The decision was soon to the advantage of the Russians, and all ran in a crowded retreat, the army moving toward Kaluga with the Cossacks in front of and beside us. The enemy army behind us shattered all the army corps, leaving each of us then without his commanding officer. Those who were too weak to carry their weapons or knapsacks threw them away, and all looked like a crowd of gypsies.

I and my fellow attendant traveled with the major as best we could. At one time my fellow attendant said, "Walter, you look all yellow in the face. You have the jaundice!" I became frightened at this and believed that my end would soon have to come, too, though I actually felt nothing.

Then we came to a second city, Borovsk. Here the city was immediately ablaze; and, in order for us to get through, soldiers had to be used to quench the flames. Camp was pitched by this city, and it became dark. One no sooner thought of resting than the Russians fell upon our army and cut off many as captives. Everything was in confusion, and during almost the whole night the throng had to retreat to Moshaisk, everyone running so as not to fall into the hands of the enemy. Because of these considerable losses, cannon, munition wagons, coaches, and baggage wagons by the hundreds had to be thrown into the water; and, where that was impossible, all wagons were burned, not one wheel being permitted to remain whole. The sutlers, even the cavalry, had to give up their horses so that these could be hitched to the cannon. The fighting, the shrieking, the firing of large and small guns, hunger and thirst, and all conceivable torments increased the never-ending confusion. Indeed, even the lice seemed

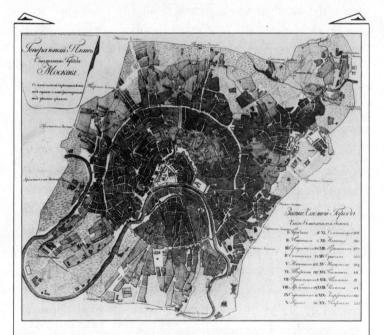

12. THIS FOLDING MAP OF THE CITY OF MOSCOW IS A REMARKABLE FEATURE OF THE 1813 EDITION OF THE RUSSIANS AND NAPOLEON BONAPARTE BY BULGAKOV. LIGHT-SHADED AREAS INDICATE PARTS OF THE CITY DAMAGED BY FIRE DURING NAPOLEON'S RETREAT. THE KEY AT THE LOWER RIGHT DIVIDES THE CITY INTO TWENTY DIS-TRICTS, SHOWING THE NUMBER OF HOUSES DESTROYED IN EACH.

to seek supremacy, for their number on both officers and privates was in the thousands.

In times when death was near, God sent me help again and again. After midnight, when we pitched camp again following the above-mentioned pursuit by the Russians, a little village stood a quarter of an hour off the highway, and I crept with my master and two horses into a stable that still had a roof. There I saw hanging on a cord behind a grate a smoked pig's head. As if received from the hand of God, I took it off from the cord with a prayer of thanks. I, my master, and my fellow servant ate it with unbelievable appetite, and we felt life come to us again. Then I always thought: "If even a few should get to German soil, it is possible that I with God's help might also reach there." In these days it snowed for the first time, and the snow remained. The cold arrived at the same time, too, and the freezing of the people multiplied the number of the dead. No one could walk fifty paces without seeing men stretched out half or completely dead. According to Napoleon's scheme we were to strike leftward toward Galicia. The Russian, however, hindered us and drove us past Vereia and Verina and to the right into our old, desolate highway.

Finally we went over the battlefield at Moshaisk in the Holy Valley. Here one saw again in what numbers the dead lay. From the battle site on to this place the corpses were dragged from the highways, and entire hollows were filled with them. Gun barrels lay one on top of another in many piles from fifteen to twenty feet in height and in width where we bivouacked for the night.

Here God once more came to my help in a wondrous

way. As I sought to fetch water in the night with my field flask, I came to a lake in which a hole had been chopped through the ice, and I drew my water with much effort because of the pressure of those standing around. On the way back, a round ball resembling a dead sheep was lying on the ground. I picked it up and in astonished joy unwrapped a rolled-up Crimean fur that reached from my head down to my feet, besides having a perculiar collar which could be clapped over my head. With my eyes turned to heaven I prayed again to God and gave thanks for the abundant mercy which I had received just when help was obviously most necessary.

I hurried to my major and had already put on the fur. He saw me and called out loudly, "Aye, God! What do you have on?" "A fur, Major, that I found just now. Now I've at least a covering." "Oh," he said, "I'll give you my fur. It's also a good one. If we get home, then you can have it back again, or I'll pay you enough for it." Thus I took his fur, which was also beautiful, having a green silk lining so that it could be worn right side out or inside out. The next morning everyone hurried on his flight, and no one wanted to be the last.

We now came to Gshatsk, and this town was already in flames. Here again many cannon were thrown into the water and part of them buried. The pressure was so frightful that I and my major lost each other. Now I had the second horse to myself, and we could not find each other again that day, nor even for another ten days.

Thus in the evening I rode apart from the army to find in the outlying district some straw for the horse and rye for myself. I was not alone, for over a strip ten hours' wide soldiers sought provisions because of their hunger; and, when there was nothing to be found, they could hunt up cabbage stalks here and there from under the snow, cut off some of the pulp from these, and let the core slowly thaw out in their mouths. Nevertheless, this time I had a second considerable piece of luck. I came to a village not yet burned where there were still sheaves of grain. I laid these before the horse and plucked off several heads of grain. I hulled them, laid the kernels mixed with chaff into a hand grinder which had been left in a house, and, taking turns with several other soldiers, ground some flour. Then we laid the dough, which we rolled into only fist-sized little loaves, on a bed of coals. Although the outside of the loaves burned to charcoal, the bread inside could be eaten. I got as many as fifteen such balls.

For further supply, whenever I came upon sheaves of grain, I picked the heads, rubbed off the kernels, and ate them from my bread sack during the course of the day. Several times I also found hempseed, which I likewise ate raw out of my pocket; and cooked hempseed was a delicacy for me because the grains burst open and produced an oily sauce; yet since I could not get salt for cooking, it did not have its full strength.

When this good night was half over, I laid four sheaves over my saddle and rode to the head of the army as usual. Toward the next night, however, in order to make a fire again, I rode off the highway. Wading in the deep snow was too hard for my horse; so I took a peasant's sled, which had only two slabs of bark for boards, put a collar made from a sack around the horse's neck, and tied two ropes from there to the sled. As I drove on again the same night, I had to cross a river about sixty feet wide, over which only four or five poles lay. I, therefore, knew of no other means than to carry the sled over on the poles and to force the horse to swim across. Accordingly I carried the emptied sled across successfully, although my feet went knee-deep into the water because the poles sank. I brought the horse, which could swim well, being of a Russian breed, to the sled again, and drove on. At this river I met a man by the name of Wittenhöfer, from my native village, who was already deathly weak. I let him ride. He died after a few days.

I continued, then, this sled-riding through the burned cities of Viasma, Semlevo, and Dorogobush without finding my master. Once, while I was eating some of my aforementioned bread, several Frenchmen saw me. These inhuman men surrounded me with the pretext of buying bread; and, when the word "bread" was mentioned, everyone bolted at me, so that I thought my death was near; but through an extraordinary chance there came along some Germans, whom I now called to my aid. They struck at my horse so that most of the Frenchmen fell back from me and then were entirely beaten off.

Among these Germans were two sergeants from my regiment called N. and N. After I was free, they took my bread and walked away. Not they, I could see now, but rather their hunger and my bread were both my redeemers and, at the same time, my robbers. Although I had already given them a loaf, they robbed me! But this, my dear readers, is to be judged otherwise than you think. There are stories in which people have murdered and eaten each other on account of hunger, but certainly this incident was still a long way from murder. Since starvation had risen to a high degree, why could not such a thing happen? And, besides that, much of the humanity of man had already vanished because of hunger. Indeed, I even heard at that time that several men had been murdered for the sake of bread. I myself could look cold-bloodedly into the lamenting faces of the wounded, the freezing, and the burned, as I shall tell later, and think of other things.

We arrived at Smolensk on November 12, having made, from Moscow to that city, 26 days and nights of travel without pausing a day. If we traveled only twelve hours daily, then we had retreated 312 hours up to Smolensk.

13. COLORFUL WOODCUT, DRAWN BY CONRAD OPPERMAN AND EN-GRAVED BY FRIEDRICH NEYER, OF AN AGITATED NAPOLEON AS A VANQUISHED NERO. FATHER TIME, SCYTHE IN HAND, DRAWS THE "FINAL CURTAIN" ON BOTH THE EMPEROR AND THE MOST OBVIOUS SYMBOL OF HIS FAILED CAMPAIGN, THE CITY OF MOSCOW IN FLAMES.

When I arrived at Smolensk, it was raining rather
heavily, and my sled could be pulled only with great effort.
When I came toward the city, the crowd was so dense
that for hours I could not penetrate into the column, for
the guard [i.e., Imperial Guard] and the artillery with the
help of the gendarmes knocked everyone out of the way,
right and left. With effort I finally pressed through, hold-
ing my horse by the head, and accompanied by sword
blows I passed over the bridge. In front of the city gate
I and my regiment, now disorganized, moved to the right
toward the city wall beside the Dnieper River. Here we
settled down and had to camp for two days. As had been
reported to us beforehand, we were to engage in battle
with the enemy here and also to get bread and flour from
the warehouses. Neither of the two reports, however,
proved to be true. The distress mounted higher and
higher, and horses were shot and eaten. Because I could
not get even a piece of meat and my hunger became too
violent, I took along the pot I carried, stationed myself
beside a horse that was being shot, and caught up the
blood from its breast. I set this blood on the fire, let it
coagulate, and ate the lumps without salt.

While we tarried two days at Smolensk, the Russians
advanced and awaited us at Minsk. Everyone hastily fled.
Cannon were thrown into the water. The hospitals were
nearly all left to the enemy; and, as was commonly rumored, the hospitals were set afire and burned with their
inmates. This is more credible when one considers the
treatment of the captured Russians; for, when we were
victors over the Russians, whole columns of captives were
transported past us, and anyone who stayed behind be-

cause of weakness and fell back as far as the rear guard was shot in the neck so that his brain always crashed down beside him. Thus every fifty to a hundred paces I saw another who had been shot with his head still smoking. All this was done to make our passage safe, so that no robber corps could be formed behind us. Very few of the captives, however, were saved from starvation.

Now, as the march went on, I had to leave my sled behind and to lay my baggage on the horse, upon which I also mounted often during the day. The cold increased again that same day, and the road became as smooth as a mirror from the rain so that the horses fell down in great numbers and could not get up again. Since my horse was a native of the country, it had no horseshoes and could always help itself up again when it had fallen. It had even the good custom, whenever we went down-hill, of sitting down on its rump, bracing its front feet forward, and sliding into the valley in this fashion without my dismounting. Other German horses, though, had shoes which were ground entirely smooth and for this reason could not keep themselves from slipping; nor could these irons be torn off, since no one had a tool for that.

Until now I had not seen my major again and be-lieved nothing else than that he must be dead. I always cared for my horse by riding out at night where some village blazed brightly, in order to get some rye sheaves for the horse and rye grains for myself. I often could not get feed for four or five days, but my "*Goniak*" [trotter] was indifferent if only from time to time he could get some old straw from the camp or some thatch straw from

a burned house, nor could I notice that he was getting
thin. If I found some rest at night, I served as a crib for
him. I always hung the halter strap on my arm or foot
so that I could notice any attempts to take him away. I
laid myself squarely before his feet; and, when he had
something to eat, he ground away with his teeth for a
short time. When he had nothing, he sniffed and snorted
all over me. Not once did his hoof touch me. At the
most he pressed my fur coat a little. Unless you tied your
horse to yourself, the horse was stolen immediately.

After leaving Smolensk, we arrived on November

14. ORIGINAL ETCHING, ONE OF A SUITE OF FORTY-THREE, DRAWN
BY THE SATIRIST AND CARICATURIST IVAN TEREBENEV (1780–1815).
HERE, NAPOLEON HAS BEEN DROPPED INTO A BARREL MARKED "KA-
LUGA ROAD," WHILE A SOLDIER AND FIREMAN STEEP TEA AS A
CHASER FOR A BAR MARKED "VIAZMA" (CITY IN WESTERN RUSSIA)
STUFFED DOWN HIS THROAT.

16, amid a thousand kinds of danger at Krasnoë, where the Russians received us, having in the meantime circled around to our front. Here the French Guard, with the remaining armed forces that could still be brought together, took its position along the highway and kept up the firing against the enemy as well as possible. Although the enemy had to yield, any movements on our part drew vigorous firing upon us. Unfortunately, all the time the greatest misery fell upon the poor sick, who usually had to be thrown from the wagons just to keep us from losing horses and wagons entirely and who were left to freeze among the enemies, for whoever remained lying behind could not hope to be rescued.

Here I once heard my master speak (rather yell) close in front of me, whereupon I called, "Major, is it you?" He glanced at me and cried out for joy, "Oh, God, dear valet, is it you? Oh, now I am glad that I have you again. Oh, I am so happy that you are still alive." I also showed my joy over this reunion, for my master still had his old German chestnut, his horse from home, and his other attendant was also with him with a second horse. Now he asked me whether I still had part of his sugar loaf and coffee. Sadly I had to say that once when I lay down behind a battlement near a fire-razed village at night a group of Cuirassier Guards pressed upon me and tore away from me the sack with the sugar and coffee; and I almost failed to keep my horse. I gave in, therefore, and chose another place to lie down, and in occupying my second spot I found straw lying about, with which my horse could still his hunger. I myself lay down on a spot that was soft and not frozen. Before departing I thought

I would see why it was so soft and warm under me, and I saw a dead man whose unfrozen belly had served as my good bed. "And I set out upon my journey again, Major, without being able to meet you again." The major then said, "That does not matter now. I am glad that you are here again."

General Ney, about whom no one knew anything anymore, was in charge of the rear guard. He fought his way through to us. However, his forces were half gone. The march had to go on; and the striking, clubbing, and skirmishing commenced so frightfully that the cry of murder echoed all about. The Cossacks advanced upon the army from all sides. We came toward Dubrovna, and the throng was so great that those on foot were usually beaten and cudgeled to the right and the left of the roadway at such narrow passages as marshes, rivers, and bridges. here my major and I were pushed apart and lost each other again. It was not possible to recognize one another except by voice. Everyone was disguised in furs, rags, and pieces of cloth; they wore round hats and peasant caps on their heads, and many had priest's robes from the churches. It was like a world turned upside down. I had had enough of my helmet at the very beginning of the retreat. I put on a round hat, wrapped my head with silk and muslin cloths and my feet with thick woolen cloth. I had on two vests and over my doublet a thick and large Russian coat which I had taken from a Russian in exchange for my own at Smolensk on the trip into Russia; and over all this I wore my thick fur. I was so enwrapped that only my eyes had an opening out of which I could breathe. From time to time I had to break off from this opening the ice that would immediately form again from my breath.

At night in Dubrovna, when the enemy had given up their maneuvers, everyone settled down in and around the place. Every night, the fires for warming could be seen over a region four hours' long and wide, reddening the sky like red cloth. The burning villages at the side contributed most to this sight, and the shrieking, beating, and lamenting did not stop for a minute. Again and again people died, and sometimes froze to death; these were people who pressed toward the fire but were seldom permitted to get there; so they died away from the fire, and very often they were even converted into cushions in order that the living would not have to sit in the snow.

In every bivouac soldiers who looked like specters crept around at night. The color of their faces, their husky breathing, and their dull muttering were horribly evident; for wherever they went they remained hopeless; and no one allowed these shades of death to drag themselves to the fire. Usually six, eight, or ten of us had to combine to build a fire, since no other wood was to be had except rafter pieces from burned houses, or trees lying around, shattered wagons, etc., and without the cooperation of the men nothing could be accomplished. Neither did we dare to fall asleep at the fire all at the same time, because no one was safe from stealing and robbery.

As we came to Orscha, it was said that we would get shoes and bread from a magazine, also oats for the horses; but this was impossible. In spite of the guards stationed around the storehouses, none of the doors could be opened, since everyone hit and shoved each other in order to get close to a door. I hurried there at first to obtain oats, but that was impossible until the guards could no longer stand their ground and the doors were sprung open. Then I climbed through a window opening, took several sacks of oats with the help of my comrades, and brought them to the camp fire. Immediately thereafter a soldier who also shared in my fire came with two loaves of bread. Now everyone's heart beat with eagerness, and everyone sprang toward the bread store. When we arrived, no one could get inside anymore, and those within could not come out because of the pressure. What was to be done? Many weak soldiers lay on the floor and were trampled down, screaming frightfully. I made for a window opening again; tore out the shutter, the wooden grating, and the window; and got five of the loaves, though they were trampled and broken. This was since Moscow the second bit of bread, for which I thanked God anew with tears.

Now we were all happy by the fire, and with renewed spirits we resumed our journey toward whatever fate had in store for us. Always I set my mind to it and constantly made my way toward the front of the army rather than to the rear. Very often I had to go back because of the Cossacks roaming about; then I joined the front of the column again so as not to be cut off from behind.

Between Orscha and Kochanova I again rode off to the side of the army toward a village which stood in flames, in order to warm myself for a short time in the night and to seek for whatever was available. No sooner had I lain down than the Cossacks came and caught whomever of us they could get. My horse had a peculiar intelligence; for, as soon as shots were fired, it turned and ran of its own accord with all its strength. In the absence of danger, however, striking it often did no good when I wanted to ride fast. Thus it saved me by flight, and we headed toward the army again. Those on foot who had also made the side march were caught and plundered. The Frenchmen were usually struck down by the Russians and not pardoned. Those who were German could reckon on pardon with certainty because, as it was said, the Russian Emperor had commanded that the Germans be spared, since the Empress, as is known, was a descendant of the house of Baden.[11]

While on my side march I saw lying on the ground a beautiful black bearskin with head and claws, which fugitives had had to throw away. With cries of "hurrah" I took possession of this in the hope of bringing my belongings to Germany, for I had various silver vessels from Moscow which were worth from three to four hundred florins. Besides this, I had silk goods, muslin, etc., such as I was able to take in abundance from the stalled wagons. Nevertheless, all this came to nothing. The retreat led through Kochanova, Toloczin, Krupky, Bobr, and Liecnize to Borissov. In the bustle by day and by night that hardly let me rest or sleep even a few hours in four or five nights, my horse, which was tied to my arm by a strap, was cut off and led away unnoticed. Since I was always accustomed to pulling on the strap on waking up to see whether my horse was still there, I pulled and this time felt no horse. I jumped up—and now what? I thought to myself, even if I had the whole night to spend looking, only a miracle could lead me to my horse, and the likelihood was all the more uncertain if my horse was already on the march. However, I had to do something. I ran left and right, back and forth; and, whenever I tried to run close to a horse, my life was endangered by whipping and beating, for one could not take enough precaution against theft and robbery: usually one of those sitting by the fire had to keep watch. All at once I saw my "*Koniak*" standing before a chapel door with his strap tied to a soldier who was sleeping inside the doorway. Very softly now I in my turn cut the strap and rode toward my fire. I dared not sleep anymore, I thought, so that if my horse lover returned I could speak with him. . . .

This night I came by chance upon a comrade from B. by the name of Sch. This was the third man from my district whom I met on the way from Smolensk to Moscow and back to this place. An officer also had this man with him as a faithful friend, for he no longer could be distinguished as "Johan" or servant [?]. Indeed, every soldier was like an officer now, since none of the uniforms showed any distinction in rank and no superior could command a private. Officers were beaten away from the fire just as privates were whenever they tried to press forward without merited claim. Only mutual support still procured true friendship. This aforesaid countryman, whom I had once liked so well, still had some rice from Moscow, though only a handful. Along with this, I had a little piece of meat which I cut off next to the ears from a dog's pelt with the whole head on it that lay not far from our fire. Just to give the water flavor and to warm our stomachs, we boiled the two together. Now, when it was only half cooked, we started eating; and, although the meat already stunk a good deal and there was no salt with it, we devoured everything with the best appetite, feeling ourselves lucky to have for once obtained something warm.

Some time before the departure, he said to me, "I had a loaf of bread for my master. You have taken it from me." This was a pain to my feelings which I can never in my life forget. It is noteworthy how an opinion which is entirely false can turn a friend into a scoundrel and change him into a shameful caricature of a human being on account of a bit of bread. Here I saw truly how low reason had sunk with us: our brains were frozen, and there was no feeling left. I swore and said, "Comrade, you are wrong. I have not seen or taken any bread. I would rather give you bread than take it." It did no good. He remained firm in his opinion, and death soon found him.

Before I came to Borissov, we bivouacked behind a forest around eleven o'clock at night, and it seemed as though the Russians had surrounded us entirely, for the cannonades thundered upon us from all sides, and it was necessary to retreat hurriedly until the enemy gave up from weariness. Everyone among us let loose with slugging, hitting, and chasing, as if we were enemies among ourselves. Every time in bivouac the Germans joined together and made the fires in groups I was also included. They were mostly Württemberg sergeants and soldiers who joined with me at the fire; and here each one fried the horse meat which he had cut off laboriously along the way often with scuffling and slugging; for, as soon as a horse plunged and did not get up immediately, men fell upon it in heaps and often cut at it alive from all sides. The meat, unfortunately, was very lean, and the only skin with a little red meat could be wrested away. Each of us stuck his piece on a stick or saber, burned off the hair in the fire, and waited until the outside was burned black. Then the piece was bitten off all around and stuck into the fire again. One seldom had time for boiling, and not one among twenty men had a pot.

When the night meal was ended here, we all lay down, and I went to sleep. My horse was tied to my arm as was my custom. In a short time one of my sincere comrades cried, "You, look after your horse so that it won't be stolen." I said, "It's here all right." I was not awakened again the second time. My countrymen cut the strap and sneaked away. Then I woke up to find myself forsaken. "God," I thought, "who is it that can save me? What is to be done? Mine and my master's possessions I cannot bring any farther. I cannot carry even my fur because of my weakness, and I must freeze to death without it." These thoughts made me despondent, and increasing pain consumed my body. Now I had to risk something even if my life should be lost; besides, it was already half gone, I thought. Only about a hundred paces away lay the French Cuirassier Guards who earlier had forcibly taken my coffee and sugar loaf while in camp. I will risk taking a horse! I crept near the front, observing which of the men did not move and might be sleeping, cut off a strap, and came away with a very large black horse. I went to a place some distance away where no one was about, then ran hurriedly to get my luggage, laid it on, and went on without delay. Indeed, I thought, if only the owner will not see me! Because of this fear, I later traded off the horse.

Before daylight, as I rode thoughtfully along, I heard my master again, Major von Schaumberg. I called him by name, whereupon he heartily rejoiced and said, "Now we are together again." He told of his preservation until now, and I also told him of mine. He was particularly glad about my care for his luggage and about my reconquest of a horse. After we came to Borissov, we bivouacked again. We came to a lumberyard and built a fire there. When the major had become somewhat warm, his "subjects" plagued him with unusual wickedness, and for this reason he asked me to kill the tormentors in his shirt collar. I did it; but, when I had his collar open, his raw flesh showed forth where the greedy beasts had gnawed in. I had to turn my eyes away with abhorrence and reassure the master that I saw nothing, telling him that my eyes hurt so much from the smoke that I could not see anything. These pests, however, were no less to be found on me, thousands of them. However, because of my constant restlessness they could not get to the point of forcing me to treat them with flesh. Besides, I remembered the saying, "Lice stay on healthy people only," and I did not count this a plague in view of the greater one.

As I walked about within the court, I saw about twenty dead cows which must have died from hunger and cold. When I tried to cut something off from them with my saber, they were all frozen as hard as a rock, and only with the greatest effort did I finally rip a belly open. Since I could cut or tear nothing loose but the entrails, I took the tallow and supplied myself with a goodly amount of

15. ENTITLED "A RUSSIAN COSSACK," THIS ENGRAVING IS BY AN ARTIST FROM MIDDLE EUROPE.

it. Each time I would stick a little of this tallow on my saber and let it get just hot enough in the fire for the greatest part of it to remain unmelted, and I would eat one piece after another with the greatest eagerness. What I had heard before—namely, that tallow-eating drove sleep away, I now found to be true. For about fourteen days I had tallow, which I always ate only in the greatest emergency and which I thriftily saved; and, truly, sleep did not bother me any more: I could always be active then throughout the night and could forage for myself and my horse in various ways.

It was November 25, 1812, when we reached Borissov. Now the march went toward the Beresina River, where the indescribable horror of all possible plagues awaited us. On the way I met one of my countrymen, by the name of Brenner, who had served with the Light Horse Regiment. He came toward me completely wet and half frozen, and we greeted each other. Brenner said that the night before he and his horse had been caught and plundered but that he had taken to flight again and had come through a river which was not frozen. Now, he said, he was near death from freezing and starvation. This good, noble soldier had run into me not far from Smolensk with a little loaf of bread weighing about two pounds and had asked me whether I wanted a piece of bread, saying that this was his last supply. "However, because you have nothing at all, I will share it with you." He had dismounted, laid the bread on the ground, and cut it in two with his saber. "Dear, good friend," I had replied, "you treat me like a brother. I will not forget as long as I live this good deed of yours but will rather repay you many times if we live!" He had then a Russian horse, a huge dun, mounted it, and each of us had to work his way through, facing his own dangers. This second meeting, with both of us in the most miserable condition because no aid was available, caused a pang in my heart which sank in me unforgettably. Both of us were again separated, and death overtook him.

When we came nearer the Beresina River, there was a place where Napoleon ordered his pack horses to be unharnessed and where he ate. He watched his army pass by in the most wretched condition. What he may have felt in his heart is impossible to surmise. His outward appearance seemed indifferent and unconcerned over the wretchedness of his soldiers; only ambition and lost honor may have made themselves felt in his heart; and, although the French and Allies shouted into his ears many oaths and curses about his own guilty person, he was still able to listen to them unmoved. After his Guard had already disbanded and he was almost abandoned, he collected a voluntary corps at Dubrovna which was enrolled with many promises and received the name of "Holy Squadron." After a short time, however, this existed in name only, for the enemy reduced even them to nothing.

In this region we came to a half-burnt village away from the road, in which a cellar was found under a mansion. We sought for potatoes, and I also pressed down the broad stairway, although the cellar was already half filled with people. When I was at the bottom of the steps, the screaming began under my feet. Everyone crowded in, and none could get out. Here people were trampled to death and suffocated; those who wanted to stoop down for something were bowled over by those standing and had to be stepped upon. In spite of the murderous shrieking and frightful groaning, the pressure from outside increased; the poor, deathly weak men who fell had to lie there until dead under the feet of their own comrades. When I reflected on the murderous shrieking, I gave up pushing into the cellar, and I thought in cold fear: how will I get out again? I pressed flat against the wall so that it afforded me shelter and pushed myself vigorously little by little up the steps; this was almost impossible with others treading on my long coat. In the village of Sembin, where Napoleon ate, there was a burned house, under which was a low, timber-covered cellar with a small entrance from the outside. Here again, as potatoes and

16. *Near Oschmaeny (Ashmiany), 4 December 1812. G. Küstner, printer. Emminger, lithographer. In desperation, the living strip the infirm of their blankets and boots, leaving them to die in the frozen wake of the retreat.*

the like were being hunted for, suddenly the beams fell in and those who were inside and were not entirely burned up or suffocated were jumping about with burned clothes, screaming, whimpering, and freezing to death in terrible pain.

When I had gone somewhat farther from that place, I met a man who had a sack of raw bran in which there was hardly a dust of flour. I begged him ceaselessly to sell me a little of the bran, pressing a silver ruble into his hand; so he put a few handfuls in my little cloth, although very unwillingly, whereupon I happily continued on my journey. When I and my master came closer to the Beresina, we camped on a near-by hill, and by contributing wood I obtained a place at a fire. I immediately mixed some snow with my bran; balled it together into a lump about the size of my fist, which because of its brittleness fell into three or four pieces again in the fire; and allowed it to heat red on the outside in order to obtain something like bread from the inside; and I and my master ate it all with the heartiest appetite.

After a time, from about two till four o'clock in the afternoon, the Russians pressed nearer and nearer from every side, and the murdering and torturing seemed about to annihilate everyone. Although our army used a hill, on which what was left of our artillery was placed, and fired at the enemy as much as possible, the question was: what chance was there of rescue? That day we expected that everyone must be captured, killed, or thrown into the water. Everyone thought that his last hour had come, and everyone was expecting it; but, since the ridge was held by the French artillery, only cannon and howitzer balls could snatch away a part of the men. There was no hospital for the wounded; they died also of hunger, thirst, cold, and despair, uttering complaints and curses with their last breath. Also our sick, who had been conveyed to this point in wagons and consisted almost entirely of officers, were left to themselves; and only deathly white faces and stiffened hands stretched toward us.

When the cannonade had abated somewhat, I and my master set out and rode down the stream for about half an hour to where there was a village with several unburned houses. Here was also the general staff of Württemberg. In the hiding places here, I sought for something to eat at night; with this purpose I lighted candles that I had found; and I did find some cabbage ("*Kapusk*") which looked green, spotted, and like rubbish. I placed it over a fire and cooked it for about half an hour. All at once cannon balls crashed into the village, and with a wild cheer the enemy sprang upon us. With all the speed we succeeded in escaping, since we mounted and rode away as fast as possible. I couldn't leave my pot of cabbage behind, to be sure, but held it firmly in my arms on the horse, and the fear that I might lose my half-cooked meal made me forget entirely the bullets which were flying by. When we were a little distance from the place, my master and I reached our hands into the pot and ate our cabbage ("*Kapuska*") in haste with our fingers. Neither could leave his hands bare because of the cold, and because of our hunger and the cold we vied with each other in grabbing swiftly into the warm pot, and the only meal for the entire day was at an end again in short time.

When it became day again, we stood near the stream

approximately a thousand paces from the two bridges, which were built of wood near each other. These bridges had the structure of sloping saw-horses suspended like trestles on shallow-sunk piles; on these lay long stringers and across them only bridge ties, which were not fastened down. However, one could not see the bridges because of the crowd of people, horses, and wagons. Everyone crowded together into a solid mass, and nowhere could one see a way out or a means of rescue. From morning till night we stood unprotected from cannonballs and grenades which the Russians hurled at us from two sides. At each blow from three to five men were struck to the ground, and yet no one was able to move a step to get out of the path of the cannonballs. Only by the filling up of the space where a cannonball made room could one make a little progress forward. All the powder wagons also stood in the crowd; many of these were ignited by the grenades, killing hundreds of people and horses standing about them.

I had a horse to ride and one to lead. The horse I led I was soon forced to let go, and I had to kneel on the one which I rode in order not to have my feet crushed off, for everything was so closely packed that in a quarter of an hour one could move only four or five steps forward. To be on foot was to lose all hope of rescue. Indeed, whoever did not have a good horse could not help falling over the horses and people lying about in masses. Everyone was screaming under the feet of the horses, and everywhere was the cry, "Shoot me or stab me to death!" The fallen horses struck off their feet many of those still standing. It was only by a miracle that anyone was saved.

In the crowd the major and I held fast to one another; and, as far as it was possible, I frequently caused my horse to rear up, whereby he came down again about one step further forward. I marveled at the intelligence with which this animal sought to save us. Then evening came, and despair steadily increased. Thousands swam into the river with horses, but no one ever came out again; thousands of others who were near the water were pushed in, and the stream was like a sheep dip where the heads of men and horses bobbed up and down and disappeared.

Finally, toward four o'clock in the evening, when it was almost dark, I came to the bridge. Here I saw only one bridge, the second having been shot away. Now it is with horror, but at that time it was with a dull, indifferent feeling, that I looked at the masses of horses and people which lay dead, piled high upon the bridge. Only "Straight ahead and in the middle!" must be the resolution. "Here in the water is your grave; beyond the bridge is the continuation of a wretched life. The decision will be made on the bridge!" Now I kept myself constantly in the middle. The major and I could aid one another; and so amid a hundred blows of sabers we came to the bridge, where not a plank was visible because of the dead men and horses; and, although on reaching the bridge the people fell in masses thirty paces to the right and to the left, we came through to the firm land.

The fact that the bridge was covered with horses and men was not due to shooting and falling alone but also to the bridge ties, which were not fastened on this structure. The horses stepped through between them with their feet and so could not help falling, until no plank was left movable on account of the weight of the bodies. For where such a timber still could move, it was torn out of place by the falling horses, and a sort of trap was prepared for the following horse. Indeed, one must say that the weight of the dead bodies was the salvation of those riding across; for, without their load, the cannon would have caused the destruction of the bridge too soon.

By the time I was in safety, it had grown dark, and I did not know where the highway was. I lay down somewhat to the left of the road in a little clump of bushes and tied the horses to my foot. The major sent a Pole after water with a kettle bought the day before and also gave him a piece of money, but the man and the kettle were never seen again, and we both had to eat the snow for our thirst. There were now so few people around that in our quiet place it seemed as though everyone had been struck dead. The cannon fire also ceased, and the bridge had really sunk, too. Horrible was the lot of the people who still were on the other side: hunger, cold, and water brought them to their death.

When in the night a little moonlight appeared, I set out upon the march again, for, on account of the cramps in my feet, I could not lie still for a quarter of an hour. Again and again I turned from one side to the other, and in the end I was frozen stiff with my clothing. Only by marching did I overcome freezing. November 26, 27, and 28.

We both hurried farther along the highway; and, being daily without bread and shelter, I thought of my friends at home and compared my misery and approaching end with my former life of plenty. I remembered a common saying at home, "A campaign is always made out to be worse than it was." With this common notion I consoled myself, thinking: "It's well that you, my beloved kindred and friends, know nothing of my condition, for it would only cause you pain, and it would be of no use to me." Yes, I thanked the Creator that only I and not my brother, too, was here. Certainly I would have lost my brother or seen him die without aid, which would have killed me as well.

I could look with indifference at the people falling by the hundreds, although the impact upon the ice bashed their heads. I could look at their rising and falling again, their dull moaning and whining, and the wringing and clenching of their hands. The ice and snow sticking in their mouths was frightful. Nevertheless, I had no feeling of pity. Only my friends were in my thoughts.

During this month the cold became worse daily. I

17. ON THE GREAT ROUTE FROM MOZHAISK TO KRYMSKAIA, 18 SEPTEMBER 1812. G. KÜSTNER, PRINTER. EMMINGER, LITHOGRAPHER.

had to be more and more careful of myself in order to keep from freezing; also keeping my horse and the major's from starving kept me busy day and night. I rode sometimes to the right and sometimes to the left in order to find a village, and load some straw or unthreshed sheaves on my horse and sit on top of them. Sitting on the straw was absolutely necessary, for otherwise it would have been stolen or torn away by the other horses.

Thus I came to Smorgoni, always keeping nearly in the middle of the army, which, however, more nearly resembled a troop of beggar Jews than one of soldiers. Here I met again, to my astonishment, well-organized regiments which came from Danzig to our support. There were two regiments of Poles who had just come back from Spain; they threw in their lot with us. A few troops came also from Württemberg, to join the Seventh Regiment, which had already been routed, likewise troops from the depot; but I did not hear of an acquaintance. Moreover, here in this region Napoleon had left us and fled with the fresh reserve troops, hurrying home ahead of the army. The general cry was, "Save himself who can." However, Murat had taken over the command of the army and remained with us. On the journey from the Beresina through Plechnizi, Slaiski, Molodetschno, and Smorgoni, I had lost the major a second time, and not until a week later did I meet him with a Württemberg captain by the name of Frost. Both were happy to have me as their attendant again.

When we approached Vilna, the cold increased still more; everyone had been forced to camp out in the snow without shelter since we had left Moscow. At night one could really see how much space the army still occupied. The fires were always visible about a two hours' march in length and about an hour's in breadth. Because of the fire and cold, the sky was a glowing red, which was increased by the burning buildings standing off the highway. Many people were almost blinded by the smoke, which did not rise because of the cold, and still others became dizzy. All our misery was reaching its climax.

When I was still a three days' journey from Vilna, about three o'clock in the afternoon the major gave me his horse, on which his coat was lying, and said that I should go just a little slowly, since he wanted to walk out a little way; and so I soon stopped and waited for him. Captain Frost and his attendant were also with me and waited, but no major came back. We waited a whole hour, and in vain. I was only too certain that he had frozen to death. What had probably happened to him was that he had not been able to put on his pulled-down trousers again because of the cold. It had been the fate of many hundreds, when they had sat down because of weakness or neccessity, that their clothing had been brutally torn from them and, where they could not defend themselves, they froze to death naked. Someone had tried this on me also, but I drove him away with a rather hard kick.

While I and the captain were still waiting for our major, the cold gripped me so terribly that I felt half-numbed. I said then, "Captain, if you still wish to wait, I'll turn the major's horse over to you. I feel that I am about to freeze, and so I am going." Then the captain left, too, and the night showed us a burning hamlet about half a mile away to the left of the highway. We hurried

toward it and warmed ourselves there till about five o'clock
in the morning. Then I heard cheering and a terrible
noise on the highway, to which I called the captain's
attention: "Let's get away; the Russians must be on the
highway."

The captain did not wish to leave the fire, and only
after strong argument did he come with me. I then had
a horse for myself, in addition to the major's horse, and
took another which stood saddled by the fire. On account
of the cold I did not ride but led these three horses by
the straps, going toward the highway. Thus we came into
the midst of the enemy on the highway. I did not have
enough strength to mount my horse, because I could not
set my feet, which were bound in rags, in the stirrups
and without the use of stirrups I was too weak to mount.
I trotted as well as I could with the horses. The Russians
called to us that they would pardon us, thinking that we
would stop and surrender. We called back, "Comrade,
pardon us," but we did not stop. Then the Cossacks rode
first at the captain and his attendant and beat them over
the heads; both fell from their horses. One also rode at
me from the left and thrust his lance into my side, and
so then I sprang to the other side of the horses. At the
same time, however, a second Cossack thrust his lance
at my neck. I let the two horses go, pulled the nearest
one aside, threw myself into the snow and the horse on
top of me; so both of us lay as if lifeless in the snow a
little off from the road. Here I rested, lying in wait with
no feeling of hunger or cold. I only kept my eyes and
ears fixed on the enemy in order to get an opportunity
to flee. I saw the beating and pushing, and heard the

whining which continued around me and could not risk making a move. All who still were standing upright were knocked down or killed. Little by little the road was emptied, since the Cossacks in front pursued the army and those behind retreated with the captives. It was my good fortune that no Cossack could plunder or expose his hands because of the cold. They had their gloves on even while thrusting their lances; that is why the first stroke at me had only passed through some of my clothes, and even the second at my neck had not injured the flesh.

After a quarter of an hour had passed, I saw it clear around me, and immediately worked myself from beneath the horse, and ran straight to the nearest wild heaths and woods on the right side of the highway. Nevertheless, in the midst of my flight I picked up a kettle with a bail on it, inside of which lay peas and a package of muslin. While I was running along in 15 inches of snow, having escaped the danger, I thought of my rescue and thanked God for His fatherly providence—all the morè so since I had obtained these peas and at the same time a cooking utensil in this lonely expanse, as though prepared by God. There was always a general need for cooking utensils, and only about one man in a hundred was provided with any. Nearly always I had to eat my horse meat, hempseed, rye, and raw grains uncooked. First of all, one had no fire; secondly, no water, having slowly to melt snow; and, finally, no utensils—usually, however, not any of all these.

In my half-joyful and half-dead condition I worked my way forward on this same day almost an hour and a half, traveling off the highway. Only the rumbling and clanging of iron tires, together with the cries of people, guided me unfailingly along my way. It grew dark, and I did not need to think: "Where will you sleep?" But as always: "The snow is your bed; and your coat and fur, your cover!" Yet suddenly I saw again a burning village about an hour's journey ahead; so I hurried to get there. When I came near, I was on my guard until I heard what language was spoken. Since I heard no more Russians, luckily, I ran to the fire. There were some twenty buildings in flames. Here I again met three men from Württemberg, and I passed the night with them.

One of them said, "If you cook your peas and if I may eat with you, I will add salt and fat," to which I gladly consented. Even without this offer I would not have been able to see my countrymen go hungry so near my

18. Near Oschmaeny (Ashmiany), 4 December 1812. G. Küstner, printer. Emminger, lithographer. The retreating soldiers fend off a Russian raiding party while birds of prey circle patiently overhead.

own unusually good dish. The fat was added, and finally we ate. When we had eaten scarcely a few mouthfuls, however, our throats burned and itched so strongly that no one was able to keep on. We examined the fat: it was soap. The food had to be thrown out, and only our hunger remained, for the peas had all been cooked. We stayed there half the night and then traveled on. The next day and also the third one, I had nothing at all to eat except some beet-juice broth I found once in a wooden tub that had a hole in the middle about three inches wide, which was unfrozen so that I could quench my thirst.

On the evening of the third day I reached the army just outside Vilna. It was in a terrific tumult. I arrived there scarcely before the Russians, who were constantly taking prisoners. Here I stood beside a mass of people who occupied all the hills in front of the city. On account of the horses and the wagons, many of them without living horses, which had piled in front of the city gates, the soldiers could not go ahead. With difficulty and with risk of life, people worked their way over the horses and wagons. Therefore, I decided to go entirely around the city and to come in from the lower side.

I was led to this undertaking by a countryman whom I met there by accident, the son of the old vine grower from Ellwangen, who came to us with the reserves. Having been acquainted with the city before, he led me into it by special paths; but in a short time I lost this good friend, too. Then I crept down a little side street into a house in which there were some Jews. I at once offered them money to get me brandy and bread. However, for my muslin, about ten yards, they offered me only a flask of brandy, about a pint and a half. I did not haggle long, because my hunger urged me to be short. I obtained the brandy, also a piece of bread, for four Polish florins and consumed everything with a ravishing appetite. When the brandy was gone, I extorted another such flask for one silver ruble but no more bread. Because I had drunk three pints of brandy within three hours, many might believe that I became terribly intoxicated, but I was far from that. Although the brandy was a decent grain brandy, I felt very little effect from it in my head, since my stomach and all parts of my body were empty and hollow and there had been no strength there before. Besides, I did not want to waste anything of this pleasure, since in my case it was a question of "Bird, eat or die!"

When the night was half gone, I started on my way so that I would not be at the rear of the army. I made my way into an enclosed court where there were many horses, untied one which was still in regular sleigh harness, and rode out of the city. About half an hour from the city there was a hill where the wagons and horses again were halted. The slipperiness of the road and the smooth horseshoes made climbing up impossible. The horses fell, and the piling up of the wagons blocked the highway so that those on foot had to climb over them. To avoid this tumult, I crossed the stream to the right and went down the valley. An hour's journey below this hill, I rode over a less steep slope back toward the highway. Because I had been so fortunate at Vilna as to obtain not only bread and brandy but also a horse, it was even harder now to face the misery once more. Hunger began again, and the cold was still just as bad as in the past days. "Truly, how many more nights will you have to endure without shelter and without fire?" I thought again and again. "My friends, how you would love to help me, and how you would long to see me again, but will it be possible?" That is what I was dreaming about all day long.

By the end of December, we reached the Polish border along the Memel River. When I heard that it would be very hard to get through near Kovno, I led my horse up the river and crossed: it was filled high with pieces of ice, really drifting ice. Pieces from 15 to 18 inches thick drifted by, so that it was extremely troublesome to climb through between them. Here the Polish army turned to the left and set out on the highway into Warsaw. I and many other Germans made use of this turn. Everyone believed that the enemy would no longer pursue the Poles on this route, and, therefore, one would be safe; but in their eagerness to rob and plunder the enemy did not stop even here. Even the Poles themselves frequently robbed and plundered the Germans and French, as I found out the same evening.

That evening a troop of riders rode up to me and said, "Comrade, stay with us!" I said, "It's all right with me." When we had gone a little further, they attacked some of the soldiers and took their horses and whatever they had. When I saw this, I turned my horse and rode back as swiftly as possible. They did not catch me again, since just then there approached a troop of Westphalian infantry, which I joined. I expected to continue to travel with these. When it grew dark, however, we looked for a village, but we did not see one. Finally, some lights blinked from the other side of the Memel. We decided to cross back, for hunger and cold made us not so afraid of danger, and we believed besides that the enemy was far away.

It really was a village. Here, for the first time since we had left Moscow, I came into a decent house, where we were warm and could have bread and brandy for our money. There were ten of us, and the villagers did not seem to be dangerous. At last, about ten o'clock, two peasants asked for bullets, telling us that they were going rabbit-hunting.

The Westphalians still had rifles and powder, and they even gave them bullets. Hardly an hour had passed before a troop of peasants stormed in, seized those who lay on the floor, and took their rifles from them. I saw no chance for help and considered besides that these were Russian peasants, who were still brutal enough to do murder.

The lights were extinguished; and in an instant I took my hat under my fur and went out the door, took my horse which was standing tied and unbridled near the door, and rode away from the village over fences and snowdrifts without following any set course, so that I and my horse fell one time after another. Sometimes I fell beneath him and sometimes on top of him.

Now I was free and left to myself again. As soon as I noticed a trail, I rode as fast as I could, for the noise in the village was so great that I believed I might still be overtaken. I rode as quickly as possible over the cracks in the ice across the Memel River in order to get to the Polish side again. The whole night now I hurried to find a village where people from the army were to be found again. Finally early in the morning, I came into a little town which was crowded with Germans, Frenchmen, and Poles. Nevertheless, I was able to get some bread.

From the Memel River to Moscow and back from there to here, I had not obtained any bread, nor could I buy it except at Vilna; and now there was an end to horse meat. I still had twenty rubles in my pocket with which I hoped to satisfy my future wants. It is true at the time of my capture I had lost silver and silk worth four or five hundred florins besides the three horses and the remaining baggage of the major. However, I did not miss this particularly, since I had saved my life. The indifference toward money was so great with me that at a point four days' journey from Vilna I did not touch a cart loaded with money which lay on the ground so broken up that the little coin barrels were rolling out. Only a few soldiers had taken any of it when I rode by. There were two reasons, though, why this money had no attraction any longer. It was nearly impossible for me to expose my hands, which were so stiff at the time that I could not feel or take hold of anything with them. I also was eager to get on so as not to be captured at the rear. This money wagon was abandoned as carelessly as any other wagon and the traces cut off. Then if the horses were still there and could be used, the men mounted them and rode on.

I hurried on, therefore, and took the highway between Königsberg and Warsaw to Thorn, where the road was thronged every day with Germans and Frenchmen. Until now there had been no thought of lodgings, nor could victuals be obtained except with money or force. One day along the road I came to a nobleman's manor-

house at which I asked for bread and obtained not only
bread but also butter and brandy, for there was a house
servant there who could speak German. He asked me my
nationality and the name of the town or village where my
home was. I told him everything, that I was a Catholic
and that the late sovereign of my country had been a
prince of the King of Poland.[12] This pleased the man
immensely, because when the Polish people knew that
one was a Catholic they esteemed him much above others.
Then I was given also several things to eat along the
way; but, when I looked for my horse, it was already
gone. Only as a particular favor on the part of the nobleman did I get it again. Nearly everyone who came
along alone with a horse had it taken from him.

Several days later, while I once more drank a glass
of brandy in an inn, having tied my horse in front of the
door, it was stolen from me. All my searching in houses
and stables was useless, and so I was set on my own feet
again. Until now my feet had been wrapped with woolen
cloth over my shoes, but because of the weight this was
a hindrance to walking. Now, every morning as soon as
I was outdoors, it was necessary to run energetically for
an hour along the way. I thought it would be impossible
to keep my feet from freezing.

Then with eight German comrades I proceeded toward Ortelsburg, where the road led through a wood that
it took almost three hours to journey through.

In this region the Poles had formed robber bands
wearing Cossack's outfits with sabers, pistols, and other
arms. A gang of these actually came and grabbed me,
one at the right, one at the left, the third setting a saber

against my breast. My comrades ahead remained unassailed, because they looked somewhat more like beggar Jews than I. Now the robbers tore off my fur, coat, cape, vests, and my head cloths; threw me to the ground; and were about to pull off my boots, too. In the meantime they found my money, to the amount of 18 rubles, in my cape pocket. This was my salvation: had they not found the money, I would have been left to freeze to death unclothed. As it was, however, they threw down the coat and the cape again along with one of the two vests and traveled off with the money, the fur, the other vest, and two head cloths. During this time my comrades kept hidden in the distance; and, when they saw that I was set free, they came running back and dressed me, for I was so stiff that I was not in a condition to dress myself.

That same evening I came to Ortelsburg and for the first time was given regular quarters. From this city I went on to Niklawi [Mlava?] and at that place received quarters again. It was just Christmas Eve, a date I would not have known if I had not learned it from the landlord. Here I also washed myself for the first time, but I could not rid myself of the lice, or rather of my "sovereigns," because if I had murdered as many as a thousand then the many other thousands would have taken revenge on me. For this reason, I did not undertake an attack on them. . . .

The washing of my hands and face proceeded very slowly because the crusts on my hands, ears, and nose had grown like fir-bark, with cracks and coal black scales. My face resembled that of a heavily bearded Russian peasant; and, when I looked into the mirror, I was astonished myself at the strange appearance of my face. I washed, then, for an hour with hot water and soap. However, I felt I had only become somewhat smoother and lighter, but I could not notice any removal of the blackness and the scales. Only where I had not been shaving did a somewhat lighter skin appear.

In this city, as in all Poland, there were also newly established regiments which had been enlisted for the reenforcement of our army. These people were on horseback, armed with lances, and had on thick coats and clothing in which hardly any of them could move about. I saw several who made a desperate effort to mount a horse, only to fall down again on the other side when they thought themselves up.

As we were departing the next day, the gate toward Thorn and Warsaw was barricaded against us, and everyone was supposed to go back to Königsberg according to the orders of the commandant of the city. This commandant acted on orders. However, we knew the condition of the army better. We were hardly outside the Königsberg gate when we all marched to the left again toward the Thorn highway, in order not to run into the midst of the enemy near Königsberg. Indeed, it cost us enough exertion to get to Thorn before the Russians; with a delay of another two days, it would not have been possible.

On the way we met a column of Bavarians who were *en route* from Königsberg to the gathering place at Plock. They told us the news that the Würtembergers, too, were gathering in Thorn and that the Germans all had permission to go home. This report strengthened my spirits again, since I had always thought that at the Vistula the army would take up its station and be reorganized and, therefore, that no one would get home or be discharged before another two years or so even if all should go well. I had been convinced of this by the enlisting in Poland.

Finally I came to Thorn; and my only silver ruble, which had escaped notice in my little watch pocket at the time I was plundered, was spent. Here I went to the town hall to obtain quarters, but could not get in on account of the mob. By chance a German soldier came along and said that on this street at a certain number there lived a commissioner from Württemberg and that he would give out passports and travel money. I presented myself immediately and obtained a five-franc thaler and a pass for the third convoy to Inowrazlav. Hence I was one of the last to come to Thorn.

The same night I lodged in a house and bought some bread and wine, for free quarters were not to be thought of. One could scarcely creep along the streets on account of the throngs of people. Early in the morning I traveled across the bridge and saw with astonishment that the city during this year of war had been developed into an important fortress. However, they had used only wooden walls and sand around the high walls. I now grew weaker and weaker, and only with great exertion did I reach the city of [Inowr]azlav. Here I reached the third convoy of our people and presented myself immediately to the commander, who asked, "Where are you from?" "From the army," was my answer. "So you are also one of those Moscow bums," he retorted, and that was the welcome at my return.

I was given arms and had to guard the park that

same night. Spending this night in the cold again gave me the fever. The next day I was even forced to continue my way on foot alone, but toward evening it became impossible. Either to die on the way or to go off to a village seen from the highway—that was my only choice. I decided then to go into the village. Here I went into a room and immediately lay down on the floor, where the fever shook me frightfully. The people there wanted to give me whiskey and something to eat, but I could drink nothing but water, and all those who looked at me made gestures of hopelessness. I naturally could not understand their conversation, but I could plainly feel their pity. In the morning I gathered together my last strength, left my arms behind because of my weakness; and only toward evening did I arrive in the station-town two hours away, where I found my convoy had already marched off again. I did not want to go to the quartering office first to obtain lodging but lay down in a tavern where there were two Westphalian soldiers who also had the fever at its worst stage. I still could not eat anything but could only drink beer, which I could get there.

The next day a citizen of the town came to the inn, too, and asked what ailed us three. He could speak German. We answered him that each of us had the fever. "The fever?" said he. "I can help you get rid of that." This he really did, sitting down, writing three notes, and saying that each of us should now eat one of them. I, at least, had little faith that such a thing could help. Nevertheless, I ate mine, too; and, when the time came for me to be shaken frightfully again, I waited longer and longer, and actually the fever left not only me but also my other two comrades at the same time. This seemed miraculous and delightful to all of us, and we thanked this good man, without whom certainly none of us would have escaped death. The next day, when we could partake of something to eat again, we obtained a wagon from the police, and I reached the convoy again outside the city of Posen. However, I was no longer able to walk from then on.

The march went on then through Posen toward Crossen. The cold was still extraordinarily great; and, since I could not walk, I froze terribly. Also at night we came into the most miserable huts where even a healthy person had a hard time bearing the cold and the smoke in the rooms with their earthen floors. The convoy consisted of 175 men. However, one or two men of this

19. BIVOUAC NEAR MIKALEWKA (MIKHALEVKA), 7 NOVEMBER 1812. G. KÜSTNER, PRINTER. THE RETREATING SOLDIERS, SOME WITHOUT BOOTS, REST AND DIE IN LARGE GROUPS BENEATH SNOW-COVERED BLANKETS.

number were brought dead to their lodgings every day. Our nourishment was still insufficient, and medicine was not to be hoped for. Although the groaning and shrieking on the wagons continued without interruption and several who were severely sick were crushed to death by the healthier people, since the space on the wagons was too small, nevertheless the impulse to help one another was still quite dulled.

As I went through Posen, I met a man from my company—among the 175 men, there was not one from my regiment, much less an acquaintance. When we recognized one another, we kissed each other for joy, and tears flowed down as each one said, "There were five of us common soldiers when we marchd out of Moscow; likely we are the last two of these left." This moved us to tears, as I said. This man from my company had been so unfamiliar to me before that I do not even know his name now. When I had to go on, he said that he was well and was just going home but not with the convoy of the sick. I learned at home that he succeeded in doing this. I had asked him, when he went home, to go through Ellwangen and give my friends the news that they could be quite certain of my return, since I was hurrying home in good health and would soon arrive.

It was still 250 leagues home; so my homecoming was still uncertain. Nevertheless, hope strengthened me always; so I finally came to Crossen, Torgau, and Leipsic, in which region German life began again, and because of decent eating and warm rooms my strength increased somewhat. In Leipsic especially I had good quarters, and everywhere there was sympathy and decent care for us.

Each of us also obtained a new shirt, and those who could walk the best also got shoes, but I obtained only a shirt. This shirt was of fine white-mangled cloth, yet is was not quite free from little shives, and not until I came to Plauen did I try to put it on. In my quarters there I took off my old shirt and laid it in the warm stove upon a few small pieces of wood in order to murder my evildoers; but, when I looked at it again, I pulled out only the shirt-sleeve: all the rest had been burned. Now what else could I do but put on my new shirt? I tried it, put it on and lay down in it, but the shives irritated me so much that I slipped into my clothes without it and exchanged it at my landlady's for a woman's shirt.

During the same night, I also learned there were in our convoy two brothers from Bernlohhof. These were of the Grenadier Company in the regiment of the Crown Prince, and one of them had died that very night. This strange chance, that two brothers who had brought themselves as far as the home stretch by supporting each other should now be separated by the death of one, is surely moving, more so for him who has a brother of his own to remember as I had.

Then the march went through Bayreuth, Nuremberg, Ansbach, and Dinkelsbühl. Everywhere we were quartered without hesitation in towns and villages. Gifts also were given us on the wagons, especially in Dinkelsbühl.

Finally, on February 24, 1813, I arrived here [at Ellwangen] with my extraordinary uniform. For such a long time I had been looking forward to my arrival at home; but, the closer I came, the more my heart pounded at the thought of seeing my friends. I would rather have arrived at nighttime; but it had to be by day, toward three o'clock in the afternoon.

My convoy from [Inowr]azlav to here had left behind 100 dead out of 175 men, and 75 men on a few wagons reached the border. Since people here already knew of the arrival of a third part of the Württemberg army, my brother and my brother-in-law, Herr Wagner, hurried toward Rettstadt to ask about me if they should not meet me. All at once I saw my brother-in-law and my brother. They would not have recognized me, of course, as I looked then; but I called, thrust out my hand, and greeted them. They jumped into the air for joy and pressed my hands, and our hearts alone could feel, for we could not speak. Oh, that all people might know how high the love of friends and relatives can mount through such a chance meeting! One feels in it heavenly joy, the all-wise providence of God, and at the same time the miracle of nature.

So my brother-in-law ran at once with powerful stride, toward the town and announced my arrival to everyone. Thus I made my entrance with a sooty Russian coat, an old round hat, and, under and in my clothing, countless traveling companions, among which were Russians, Poles, Prussians, and Saxons. I stopped off at my very good friend's, the innkeeper's. Everyone wanted to lift me down and lead me, and everyone regarded me as weaker than I really was. However, I stayed only a few minutes in the room before I took off my clothes in the haymow, put on the new ones already provided for me, and washed myself. Only then was I fit for clean company.

Now I also awaited my dear sisters, who did not

come in from Rosenberg until the following day and were another object of joy. The sincere joy of meeting again kindled the love of kindred as a divine flame, and now the wish was fulfilled for which they had shed so many tears and had so often prayed to God.

The next day, on Shrove Thursday, a rest day was observed upon the request of the innkeeper; he brought it about through the city commandant, Alberti, who often came to the tavern. I now had good eating and drinking, but my stomach could not stand many things as yet. I had to be quite careful all the time. On the third day, when we had driven on again, we came to Schorndorf in the evening and were shut into a house together so that we should spread no sickness, for everywhere in Württemberg we were shunned like lepers.

When we came to Waiblingen, the transport was divided, and those who were in better health, of whom I was one, went to Waldenbuch; those whose health was worse went to Vaihingen-on-the-Enz. After a fortnight I was detached to Asperg as a convalescent and was incorporated into the sharpshooters who were stationed there then, and I marched out several times with them. Barely four days had gone by, however, before the fever shook me again, although it did not break out. I ran a high temperature; and my nosebleed grew so bad that for several days a wet cloth had to be put around my head and neck every five or six minutes and the bed had to be arranged for sitting up instead of lying down; but, since my illness got worse, I was examined by the general army physician as to my physical condition, and leave was granted to me on account of my arm, which had been hurt at the time of my capture, having been wrenched somewhat in the shoulder blade and reset. At the same time an invalid pension was also promised me.

When I had grown so weak that I became delirious and everyone doubted that I would recover, I was loaded upon a wagon with several "Russians" and driven to Vaihingen. I was now so weak that I had to be lifted into and off the wagon and I could take nothing any more but drinking water. In Vaihingen I was laid immediately in the room where all were brought who were near death. No medicine or food would stay with me. However, the bleeding had stopped.

Finally, after eight or nine days had passed, I longed for vinegar, and I poured some of it into my soup. These few spoonfuls of soup stayed with me, and now my desire increased for vinegar and lettuce. The lettuce also stayed with me, although I had to take it secretly without the doctor's knowing about it. My appetite gradually rose so that I had potato salad, pure vinegar, pork, potatoes and cabbage, and cooked meat from the butcher brought to me secretly, and then I took no more medicine. I could attribute my recovery to nothing else than the bleeding, by which the corrupted blood came from me, and to the vinegar, which washed off the encrusted lining in my body, cleaned my blood, and encouraged my appetite again.

When my relatives and friends heard of my illness, my little or younger sister, greatly worried, came to visit me, in two days traveling thirty hours. All the sick were in the castle, and the fathers and mothers were kept from entering by the guard. All of them had to go away again without being permitted to speak with their sons. This caused my sister great pain, and she could not weep enough about it; yet chance and luck made a secret meeting possible, for my sister waited until the time when Sharpshooter Seybold from Hohenberg came to the post at the outer gate. He gave her permission to speak to me near the castle wall at the left and sent secretly and had someone ask me to come out. When I saw my sister and she saw me, it took a long time for her to stop weeping and to speak. My appearance had frightened her terribly, for I was deathly pale, my coat was full of blood, and my voice, deep and weak; but, when I said that I thought myself out of danger, since I felt almost well and could eat everything, she was somewhat comforted. However, the fear that she might not be allowed to speak with me had made her almost more ill than I thought myself to be. Thus we tarried as loving brother and sister for an hour's time and then parted again with tears.

During a period of two weeks I still had violent attacks of gout in the soles of my feet as well as a strong headache, and yet I did not take the medicine but always told the physician that I was well now. However, he did not believe me but said that I must have a headache and gout in my feet, in which I agreed with him, but only in my thoughts.

Finally, I was again brought as a convalescent with about 70 men to Waldenbuch to the convalescent hospital and was quartered on the way in a village, but because of the fear of the nervous fever we all had to go to the town hall and were not supposed to go out. This was hard on us, always to be treated like lepers. We went, therefore, into the inns and had some fun. It did not last long, though, until the citizens wanted to storm us, with alarms ringing and with the threat of bringing the militia from Stuttgart if we would not go back to the town hall at once. There was nothing left but to give in and to accept scorn as our reward.

At Waldenbuch Castle I more or less got my strength back, since I bought what I wanted in addition to my regular diet. Then I wrote a letter to Lieutenant Stimmer at Asperg, asking him to help me in getting my promised discharge. This was done, too, since the colonel in the hospital told me that if I wanted to go I could call for my discharge from Herr Stimmer.

At once I went through Stuttgart and toward Asperg; but, as I came to the first village in the direction of Ludwigsburg, I suddenly got such a pain in my foot that I had to walk an hour instead of a quarter hour to get to the village. Several people who saw me and recognized me as a "Russian"—as everyone who had been there was called at that time—gave me presents. Finally I came to the mayor's house and was given a conveyance to Asperg. I obtained my discharge and had myself driven home, where I then in a short time became entirely healthy and well.

Historical

Appraisal

of

Walter's

Chronicle

BY LONG-APPROVED PRACtice, writings recovered from the past are usually given a historical introduction to the public. This practice sagely recognizes that such writings have become identified with the past, or by virtue of their age have themselves a past; hence they need to be viewed historically. First, caution requires that the trustworthiness of the document be validated by test of historical criticism. Then, curiosity asks that the content of the document be elucidated and appraised by the aid of special historical knowledge. The need of such a commentary is most obvious where the nature or motive of a document is inherently historical, or where historical factors have influenced its finding and publication.

In the testing of historical evidence a first question, regularly, is how it came to light. The story of the finding of the Walter manuscript is related here for this reason. However, the story has significance for yet other reasons. The chance which brought it to light should suggest the possibility of other discoveries under like circumstances. That it should have turned up when it did, and where it did, shows the persistence of such material even in Kansas. Indeed, because of the unity and reach of Europeanism, which has contributed to the peopling of the inmost region of America, the discovery of sources for European history and culture may well be expected anywhere. The finding of such new records is a normal feature of historical study, with its constant exploring of the abundant mysteries of the past. The thrill of uncovering such treasure-trove is most often the reward of tireless research, but it can come as a chance by-product of routine teaching. Such was my experience in the autumn of 1932 in connection with a course in nineteenth-century European history. The introductory lectures had stressed the revision of current notions of the historical situation at the opening of the century, hence had dealt with the downfall of the first Napoleonic empire, and this incidentally had involved some reconsideration of the tragic campaign of 1812 in Russia. Necessarily much stress was laid upon the restudy of sources and the importance of new material, such as had been ferreted out that summer in European archives. Thereby a member of the class was led to tell of a reputed diary of the Moscow retreat, a treasured heirloom of a nearby Kansas farmstead, and thereafter I had an opportunity to examine the document.

A first critical examination of the heirloom showed that it was a German soldier's account—partly in two versions—of campaign experiences during 1806 to 1813, under Napoleon. With it was a letter of family information written in 1856 by the Napoleonic veteran to an emigrant son in America, whose grandson, Mr. Frank Walter of Lecompton, Kansas, is at present heritor of the papers. It was possible to separate, and put in order, the several versions and portions of the narrative, and to give a report upon this and the letter. But since the narrative was written in old script and in dialect, the edition of the manuscript had to wait upon the coming to the University of Kansas, from the very locality of the Swabian soldier, of Professor Otto Springer. He received with enthusiasm information about the Walter manuscript, and his special knowledge and assiduity have now resulted in the publication of the Walter story.

The circumstances having thus placed historical responsibilities for the Walter manuscript upon its discoverer, the first concern has been to apply tests of historical validity in so far as handicaps of distance and lapse of time would permit. On the point of authorship, family tradition affirmed that the Jakob Walter of Ellwangen in Württemberg, who wrote the paternal letter of February 17, 1856, to his son Albert, in America, was the same Jakob Walter who wrote the accounts of his Napoleonic war experiences. This tradition was presumably confirmed by the script and style and internal evidence of the papers themselves. A proper chance for supplementing this evidence seemed to be offered by the wish of the Kansas descendants to reestablish communication with German kindred. Through the German Embassy at Washington and the Army Archives at Stuttgart the identity of the soldier Jakob Walter was established, and incidental reference was made to his having received an 1812 service medal. The last of the kindred whose age and situation might have afforded knowledge of personal details had recently died. The Ellwangen city officials from their records could supply little but family-registry information, which largely confirms, and slightly amplifies, the data found in family letters at Lecompton.

Despite certain discrepancies in our data it can be assumed that Jakob Walter was born in 1788 in the village of Rosenberg near Ellwangen. In one version of the 1806 campaign his age is given as nineteen, but our letter of 1856 gives his birthday as May 21, 1788. In the registry record September 28, 1788, is given for his birth; August 3, 1864, for his death. His parentage is recorded: Johann Walter of Rosenberg and Eva Dietz of Bartenstein. His wife, to whom he was married on February 11, 1817, was born on May 22, 1799, and died on April 28, 1873. There were ten children from this union, five of whom were living in 1856 when the letter of that year was written. In 1858 a daughter died, and in 1861 a son. The registry does not record the deaths of the two sons who had emigrated to America or the death of the last surviving daughter in Ellwangen. All the evidence agrees that Jakob Walter was trained as a stonemason, and in 1856 he was still working at his trade as a contracting builder or overseer. He was a strong Catholic and his narrative implies that he had at least a parochial schooling. However, on this question as on almost all personal matters other than military experiences actual information is lacking.

The sons who emigrated to the United States were Franz Patritz, born in 1831, and Albert, four years younger. Franz emigrated in 1849 and was for a time at New Orleans. In 1854, at Lima, Ohio, he took out naturalization papers. Then in the spring of 1856 he settled in Douglas County, Kansas, at the territorial capital of Lecompton. He made a visit to the homeland in 1857, and during his visit married the daughter of the mayor of a village near Ellwangen. This event happened on February 22, 1858, and the fact that the day was Washington's birthday was mentioned in the wedding sermon. That same year he returned with his wife to Kansas, where on January 14, 1898, at Lecompton, his death occurred. It was on the return of Franz Walter in 1858 from Ellwangen, according to family tradition, that the accounts of the father's campaigns were brought to Kansas, as were also the parental portraits, one of which, representing the veteran at the age of fifty, is reproduced in this publication.

Regarding the manuscript itself, questions arise which might be dealt with more satisfactorily if we knew more definitely the circumstances of the bringing of the Jakob Walter manuscript to Kansas. Inferences, however, do warrant fairly certain dicta regarding the "original" character of the Walter chronicle. It is a document of some 200 pages, about eight by six inches in size. It is handwritten and a number of exacting studies of the script, involving a comparison with available signed letters, indicate that Jakob Walter was the writer throughout. He apparently used a letter paper of ordinary rag stock without watermarks, mostly handruled with pencil. The document was not bound or fastened together as a whole; instead it was organized as some eight or nine units, composed of a variant number of double sheets, each unit sewed in simple notebook fashion by the author. Naturally this arrangement disregards the division of the story into three campaign episodes, told as units, and having separate titles, but not deemed sufficiently distinct to require starting each campaign on a fresh page. Actually all the units save one, when put together, constitute a complete story as here published. The additional unit of 48 pages seems to be the starting of a second draft or "revised version" of the chronicle, covering the first and most of the second campaign, written somewhat more precisely and with some variations in the choice of details. It was not deemed practicable to publish it here; but its existence is mentioned because its presence with the other version suggests that Franz probably was given all his father had written of formal recollections. It also has pertinence to the question why and how Jakob Walter wrote his story.

On the basis of meager data, we follow up our inquiry as to the origins of Walter's manuscript. Where was it written? His reference to going home in 1813 might offer a clue. Yet it is uncertain what he referred to as home. If he had living parents they are not mentioned. His unnamed brother and two sisters evidently were dear to him. The brother's home in 1813 is unknown; the sisters, one of them married, lived at the paternal village of Rosenberg. His godfather, who had provided him with a trade, kept an inn at Ellwangen where Jakob Walter mentions staying at times. Yet would conditions at Rosenberg or at the inn have encouraged the young invalided soldier with his training as a stonemason to become an author forthwith? Would not circumstances have been more favorable after he had married, fixed his home at Ellwangen, and found his place in civil life? This opens the question of when, between 1813 and its removal to Kansas in 1858, Jakob Walter's undated narrative was actually written. Where the range of time is so long, naturally the possibility of arguments for various dates is large. There are reasons for noting some of these arguments, hereafter, for the light they throw upon the value of Walter's contributions, but it seems best, at the outset, to state that it is most probable the chronicle was written at a date between 1820 and the early 1840s and not unlikely around 1830.

The argument which weighs against a dating after 1840 is the argument of the effects of advancing years on memory and facile composition. Thus, in Walter's case, a letter written to a son in 1848 is in a cramped hand quite different from the generally easy, flowing script of his military recollections. On the other hand, the case for a dating prior to 1820 rests primarily upon the freshness of the narrative, its vivid detail, and its general reliability, especially in its geographic data, even where obscure Polish and Russian places are mentioned. These are charcteristic features of the 1812 story, and the accounts of the campaigns in 1807 and 1809 are also vivid, and, in places, surprisingly accurate. To be sure, circumspect analysis does show that the time-factor need not have affected greatly the strength of Walter's memory for certain types of data or experiences. In any case maps and some other source material must have been used for checking assertions and spellings. Also there are some factual lapses throughout, as demonstrated in my historical annotations for each of the three campaigns, and these are most noticeable for the 1809 campaign, which was fought almost at home and only three years before the Russian campaign. Is not this surely a point bearing

upon the hypothesis of an early writing of the chronicle—
a point which cannot be discounted easily? The complete
silence regarding events after 1812 presents another difficulty. If Walter wrote before 1820, it was during the
course of such a crowding train of events as must have
affected the thinking of anyone recounting Napoleonic
war-memories. The War of Liberation in Poland and
Germany had begun before Walter's return to Württemberg at the end of February 1813. When, after some
weeks of critical illness from typhus, he got his final
discharge, the spring campaign in Silesia, Saxony, and
part of Prussia, so familiar to him, was already opening.
The great events of the summer, and the fateful autumn
battles around Dresden, Reichenbach, and Leipsic, were
in regions he knew well. He cannot have been untouched
by the events which in 1814, and again in 1815, marked
the overthrow of Napoleon, and the coincident reshapings
of Germany and all Europe down to 1820. The probable
speed of Walter's writing must of course be taken into
account. We can hardly assume that he composed rapidly,
considering that he lacked training and favoring conditions, that at the outset he had to find his place in civil
life, and that he was working at a tiring trade which would
afford little incentive or leisure for authorship. It is unlikely that our manuscript is the very first draft, for the
revisions are relatively few and are in the nature of re-
touchings of an established version. It is also significant
that we have both a basic version and part of a revision.
Besides, our manuscript does reveal by its changes of
pen, ink, and script that it was written in stints, with
attendant interruptions. There is, indeed, an obvious sin-

gleness of purpose about the narrative which may indicate
a predetermined exclusion of all matter or allusions not
absolutely pertinent to Walter's own military experiences.
This is admirable, but its very rigidity suggests it is the
outcome of an experimental period of writing or retelling
of his experiences during which his story was gradually
clarified and given a definite form. The natural conclusion
is that our Walter manuscript is a product from the time
1820–40, which was a period of relative quiet for men
of maturing years and with some craving for the respect
of their posterity. Then, while the "great era" was being
seen with better perspective, personal memories of that
era were taking shape and color, and Napoleonic war
veterans were publishing enough to refresh memories and
afford useful data and literary models for other veterans,
such as Jakob Walter. Although we have no positive
evidence on the point, it is a logical inference, and highly
probable, that he too recounted his experiences primarily
from memory. Possibly some letters or other scraps from
the 1807 and 1809 campaigns had been preserved by
relatives, but this seems unlikely. Letters were written
home during the Russian campaign; Arthur Chuquet published a volume of such French letters. Some diaries kept
during the retreat were saved. All such instances, however,
so far as known, involved officers, almost all of them men
of rank and culture. Walter's is the unique example of a
private soldier. It is doubtful if he wrote home during the
entire 1812 campaign. He admits his kindred got word
of his homecoming only by indirect report. Yet, though
he had no personal papers to use, this circumstance need
not exclude the chance of his having had access to other

Moscow-campaign sources. It is well known that local newspapers for some years after 1812 carried notices of various sorts and even printed accounts of incidents connected with the campaign. We know that several important survivors of the retreat were fellow-citizens of Jakob Walter for years. Surely there were reunions of veterans or other chances for comparing experiences. Maps were available; possibly even route lists were extant. In time there were published narratives of the Russian campaign; a few appeared from 1814 to 1820, but not in German. A smattering of personal recollections came out during the 1820s, the 1830s, and the 1840s, including some written in German and published in Germany, although it is doubtful whether most of them, if any of them, would have been known to Walter.

Significantly the Walter manuscripts show evidences of the insertion of place names, distances, etc., after the original writing. The underlining of many names, especially of Polish and Russian towns, suggests also that words so marked had been filled in, or at least verified. From careful inspection our document seems to be not an initial draft but a meticulous copy. Certainly it is written with remarkable care, and alterations are relatively few. That it evidently was not deemed definitive, our partially finished "revised" version demonstrates. But the revisions do not change our initial assumption that Walter wrote primarily from memory.

What, then, of Jakob Walter's memories? The question forthwith shifts our point of attention. We turn from a critical inquiry regarding the origins of our document—the issues of authorship and sources, of time, place, and method of writing—to an analysis of its content; from a consideration of its authenticity to an examination of its reliability. Our procedure may well be by a comparison of the accounts of Walter's three campaigns. On a first reading there may seem to be little difference in the historicity of these accounts. Certainly one would hardly expect that the difference of but three to six years would cause a marked variation in the dependability of one's memories. The natural assumption, then, is that if there are marked differences in the quality of the three stories, this must be owing to factors other than the mere differences in elapsed time. Walter's actual age during each campaign must be considered in connection with the fact that the difference of interests, and thus of experiences, at each particular age must result in different sorts of memories. In this connection one must bear in mind the influence of strong, abnormal experiences in the rapid maturing of youth. Thus Walter himself, writing as if from the vantage point of more than just six years, speaks of the youthful irresponsibility of 1806. The story of 1809 reflects a sort of mocking recklessness. The strange combination of piety and casual *sauve qui peut* indiscipline of 1812 is something quite different still. There are other general differences in the accounts, due perchance to the less observant age of Walter during the earlier campaigns and to his greater indifference at the time, or perhaps to an intentional subordination of the earlier part of his military service to the more vital experiences of 1812.

If we turn to the issue of factual accuracy we shall find that a comparative test for the three campaigns yields surprising results, which incidentally bear little or no relationship to factors likely to guide us in dating the Walter narrative. Broadly speaking, the 1812 story, which we are best able to check because of the mass of other evidence, best meets the tests of good history. It hangs together best, and has most factual detail and fewest errors. That is not strange, of course, as it was Walter's last campaign, although his story of it affords no sure clues as to how recent it had been. What *is* strange is that the story of 1809 is least satisfactory historically. It is least coherent and its recital of events is most tangled and inexact. Yet it gives more fresh evidence, apparently not elsewhere available, than does the 1812 narrative, and its details are sometimes more precise and important. It is also significant that it deals with an episode regarding which secondary works are generally silent. Also such personal memoirs as are most abundant for 1812 are here lacking, and available official materials are relatively meager. For testing purposes, therefore, dependence has had to be placed upon a type of evidence less available for the 1812 critique, that is, newspapers and local monographs. For testing the 1806–7 narrative, available sources were newspapers, personal (official) correspondence, some memoir material, and some special studies. Such material has shown that, in part, Walter's recollections for this time are quite confused, but to a considerable extent are more vivid, more detailed, and surer than those of his two later campaigns. As further demonstration that the historicity of Walter's memories is not clearly relative to the closeness of events may be cited types of detail almost equally dependable for each of his campaigns.

Particularly is this the case for the campaigns of 1807 and 1809. Citation of typical examples from the Russian campaign, however, may contribute to the appreciation of that most vital portion of the Jakob Walter manuscript.

The amount of specific detail in Walter's narrative of 1812 is rather surprising. To be sure, much of it is of experiences of sufferings deeply scarring the memories of all survivors, and often the incidents and ideas in different accounts are so very similar that one would suspect borrowings of one narrative from another or from a common model were not proofs of originality incontestable. But there are authentic details peculiar to each individual narrator. In the case of Walter it is a memory of dimensions and of construction details, as natural for a builder to retain for an indefinite time, as a long memory of horses and transports was for Coignet, or the memory of minutiae of his hospital cases was the Roos [an army doctor whose memoirs are available only in German]. This type of recall is equally noticeable, just as is the surprising recollection of route-of-march details and place names and data, in each part of Walter's narrative. In the narrative of his movements there are a few serious lapses. These are less serious, but more numerous, for 1812, but then the route was far longer and more complicated. A remarkable feature of his narrative for 1812, surely, is his recall of amazingly difficult names of very minor places. But this feature must be interpreted with caution. Many of us can testify to lifetime recollections of ordinary travels, even down to small details. Walter's campaign probably marked the full scope of his travels. They were made within those years of his life when memory presumably is most impressionable and most retentive. He lived only some fifty years thereafter, within which time, it is not illogical to say, his "travel-memory" should have been reliable. The Moscow campaign was indelibly memorable as have been few episodes of history. Its route is traced, with natural variations, in detail, by most of the recitals of its survivors. Many of them are accompanied by maps, a few by atlases. Most extraordinary for minutely photographic recollection of all route details are the Bourgogne *Memoirs* of 1835, when the author had reached an advanced age. True, Bourgogne had his notes of 1814 and 1815 as controls, but indications of the use of some verifying data by Jakob Walter have been cited already. Even so, Walter is not impeccable. He has corrected some slips, made in writing or copying, where sections of his route were out of time or place sequence, but has overlooked some others. Examples of such often very natural confusion are in his narrative of his moves just before and after the Beresina crossing, also his account of the sector just east of the Niemen both on his advance and retreat routes. While his memory for names of obscure places has been cited as remarkable, it is sometimes a confusing factor. Thus footnotes, based on use of Napoleonic marching orders and on other detailed researches, have been needed to amplify and clarify Walter's itinerary through East Prussia. Because his route missed the larger places, usually, and because as a common soldier he did not know the strategy controlling his movements, his lists of century-old village names, often without essential dates, are a cause of grief to his readers. In his use of dates Walter is as dependable as any of his com-

rades who did not keep diaries. Events which he connects
with memorable days—such as church holidays—he dates
accurately, even as others do. His use of round numbers
is apt to be careless. A greater weakness, however, is a
tendency to omit dates entirely, and this tendency un-
derlies the confused accounts of his movements during
the first months of 1807 and during the Vorarlberg campaign in 1809. Yet the net result of the critical analysis
reflected in this discussion of the historicity of the Walter
chronicle has been to impress the writer—and he hopes
the reader—with its general reliability as historical evidence. Veracity, however, is but one test of the value of
a historical document.

In beginning this introduction, I referred to the
peculiar circumstances of the bringing to light the Walter
narrative as suggesting reasons why it should be of special
interest. For one thing it is highly suggestive, for those
interested in our European cultural background, that even
in Kansas documents of the Napoleonic era—and also
of the Thirty Years' War—have turned up in this fashion.
Secondly, there is interest and significance in the fact that
the Walter chronicle was brought to Kansas in early
territorial days, because heretofore study of the peopling
of this central commonwealth has concerned itself so
generally with the struggle of free- vs. slave-state elements
that foreign factors in the population at so early a stage
of Kansas history seem to have been neglected. Evidently
the Germans have played a larger part in molding the
eastern section of the state than has been realized, and
it would be profitable to know whence and why they came
and what they actually contributed. However, the pub-

lication of the Walter manuscript has been prompted chiefly by other motives, above all a realization of the interest and value of its contents for students of language and history and for the general reader because of its intrinsic human interest.

The inherent appeal of that type of writing to which the Walter chronicle belongs has already been noted. The number of such memoirs of Napoleonic war veterans, published since 1900, and still appearing despite the competition of the World War and its literature, is remarkable. But a new narrative is expected to have other particular claims of interest. The Walter manuscript does have these—both literary and historical. Its special claim, however, is that it is seemingly unique among the mass of 1812 narratives as the personal record of a German *common soldier* in Napoleon's Grand Army. But while it is largely devoted to the Russian campaign, it is actually the record of a conscripted private of a Napoleonic vassal-state. Presumably he is typical of his group, the more so because his "military-service-time" covers practically the full period of the New Charlemagne's domination of Germany and most of Europe.

The factors of Jakob Walter's personality and background have merited emphasis here. They are essential considerations in reading, with full appreciation, this relation by Walter of the military experiences of his three campaigns. He was merely a builder's helper, when called up with many like him, in the conscription of 1806, for "the campaign which the Emperor Napoleon with the princes then his allies was conducting against Prussia." This passage (omitted from the second version) is the extent of "political" allusion in the manuscript. Evidently when his regiment marched off in the fall, the Jena-Auerstädt battle (October 14) had just demolished the façade of Prussia potency. There was little for the new auxiliaries to do, after Frederick William had sought the safest corner of his realms, except clean up the remnants of unyielded defenses, in Silesia and Pomerania. During the shifting of forces between these two provinces parts of West Prussia were crossed by Württemberg regiments; but they had no part in the big fighting of the Eylau-Friedland campaign, were never exposed to the kindling close influence of the major leaders. The Walter brothers did their bit in the marchings and requisitionings incidental to various sieges and sorties here and there. Jakob had small chance and less incentive to discern any obvious scheme in the campaign. The incidents he best remembered were rowdy pranks. For the poor discipline of certain Württemberg units was such that the King at the home-coming review addressed them as his brigands. Moreover, when in 1812, the humiliated Crown Prince had to notify his father of his troops' disorders on the Prussian-Lithuanian march, which had earned Napoleonic wrath, he recalled their misconduct of 1807 in Silesia. Nevertheless those especially interested will find some enlightening contributions regarding the futile Colberg and Glatz sieges, and the general reader will enjoy some vividly portrayed sortie incidents. Quite incidentally also Walter slips in some sound observations on the condition of Jews and peasants in Poland and Brandenburg. They illustrate that personal revelation which will be found the primary appeal and significance of the document.

From the end of 1807, when Jakob Walter went on leave to be with his sisters at Rosenberg, he worked intermittently at his craft until recalled to active service in the Austrian War. Again he missed the major conflict; again he served in a side campaign too much underrated by historians. His contingent was sent to the Alpine frontier to repel attacks of insurgent peasants who were fighting to get back under their old Habsburg rulers. Therefore, instead of sharing in the Ratisbon campaign of April and the May-July battles (Aspern, Wagram) near Vienna, the Walter brothers were only in local brushes at the Vorarlberg corner of the Lake of Constance. As the second and fuller version of this campaign is incomplete, we have but a scrappy account of Walter's experiences. It shows him as more mature and taking a more soldierly part, as being more interested in people, folkways, and rural economy, perhaps as less devoutly Catholic. The disorders of his contingent seem to have changed likewise. There is little boyish rowdyism but some drunken rioting—despite their being on their own borders. Fortunately the campaign was not long, and after some garrison months Jakob Walter could again return to civil life and his trade at Ellwangen for something over two years.

Truly Walter's third campaign was one of the most momentous in history. His unit being under Marshal Ney for most the advance, he was in the thick of events. Out of that Grand Army of some 600,000 who about June 25, 1812, crossed the Russian border, he was one of the small number who survived the retreat, recrossed the Niemen in late December, and finally reached home.

Naturally the account of his 1812 experiences, about three-fourths of his manuscript, is most detailed, systematic, and vitally—even vividly—interesting. It merits recognition among the many notable memoirs of the Moscow campaign. For many memoirs available for such study, comparative ranking is impracticable because of difference in scope, motive, or nature, and because of the author's status. Bourgogne, Castellane, Caulaincourt, Fain, Marbot, Roos, and Ségur are examples. But among those of a type more similar to Walter's, such as Coignet, Lossberg, Steinmüller, Vossen, Yelin, etc., the Walter narrative surely takes high rank.

Necessarily the scope of 1812 literature forces its students to be selective, to adhere to a dominant interest or motive. With many the interest is broadly historical. They are concerned with the causes or consequences of the Russian War, its diplomacy, its strategy. For them the sources have been often exploited and digested in scholarly monographs. Some aspects will always be disputed, and some phases of diplomacy, or military topics such as the facts regarding commissariat or hospitalization, may still be live issues. As to these the soldier memoirs may add something, but as to strategy or diplomacy rarely anything fresh. Then a second group of students have a "moral" or propagandist objective. They may be seeking to demonstrate the virtues of patriotic popularism, the vices of despotism and its nemesis, the horrors and futility of war. Honest study of the evidences—including soldier memoirs—may well correct certain of their preconceptions which have become popular legends. They will find from Walter very little about peasants who attacked with flails and scythes, and that little chiefly about defending their villages and themselves against marauders. Of Cossack attacks, they will discover that most were against stragglers during the last stage of the retreat in Lithuania and Poland or East Prussia. They may learn that when Napoleon left his army at Smorgoni he had not only strong justification for rushing back to Paris, but also good reasons to turn the survivors over to capable sub-commanders, he himself having brought them into touch with supply bases, reinforcing new troops, and allied frontiers. But there is a third and most numerous group of readers motivated by the human-interest appeal, being concerned with dramatic incidents and with character portrayal. To them especially Walter's narrative is commended. His experiences are varied and representative, and particularly significant not merely as those of the army rank and file, but because of Walter's emotional revelations, thoughts of religion and the ties of home, and a persistent concern over the barbarizing effect of the retreat on himself and others. His mixture of Catholic piety and selfish energy was perhaps typically South German, yet it does show strikingly how the will to live and fend for oneself, joined with some degree of human kindness and providential aid, worked together to bring even a remnant safe home from Moscow in 1812.

Notes to the Diary

1. Count Dominique René Vandamme (1770–1830), French general.

2. *"Kapuke"* (also *"Kapusk,"* *"Kapuska"*)—probably a misunderstanding of *kapusta*, Polish and Russian for cabbage.

3. *"Bopen"*—from Russian *pop* (pl. *popy*), parish priest in common language.

4. Known as the battle of Borodino by the Russians and as the battle of the Moskova by the French.

5. French Guard, or the Imperial Guard *(gard impériale)*, the elite regiments of Napoleon.

6. Alia—possibly the Selnia River.

7. In fact the rivulet Neglinnaia, which used to be a tributary of the Moskva River—now covered over.

8. In fact the reverse was true: Alexander I ignored Napoleon's approach for an armistice or peace negotiations.

9. Apparently Napoleon gave the order to blow up the Kremlin, but it was either foiled or not carried out.

10. Glauber salt—sulphate of sodium, a laxative.

11. Princess Maria Luisa of Baden married Alexander I and took the name of Elizaveta Fedorovna.

12. There is no historical evidence for this statement.

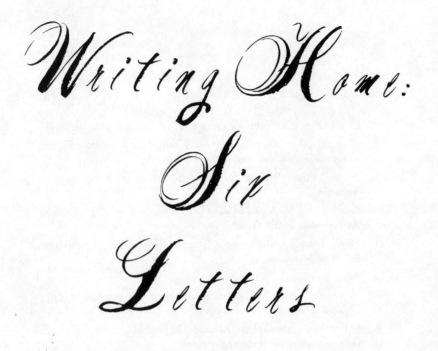

Writing Home:
Six
Letters

NAPOLEON SET UP THE Kingdom of Westphalia in 1807, and appointed his brother, Jérôme king. Like all member states of the Confederation of the Rhine, Westphalia had to provide recruits to Napoleon's armies. The Westphalians served in the French Army first during the Spanish campaign. Naturally, they were also called upon to participate in the campaign of Russia. They formed the Westphalian Corps, under the command of General Vandamme, and later under that of Marshal Junot (Duc d'Abrantès)—King Jérôme was with the corps in the beginning stages of the campaign. Several additional Westphalian units were attached to various other corps. All told, the Westphalians numbered 27,000 men at the outset of the campaign of Russia.

Napoleon was one of the first to make large-scale and effective use of what we call psychological warfare; and he did it with the populations at home in view. His famous *Bulletins de la Grande Armée* served that purpose and, naturally, gave the most optimistic accounts of victories, captured trophies, progress of the campaign, weakness of the enemy. And when the going went from bad to worse, the *Bulletins* camouflaged the disasters as much as possible. To preserve the credibility of the official news, all correspondence from the front lines was censored. Letters that would have contributed to demoralizing the home front, or that would have reflected the hardships and horrors of the campaign were confiscated. Some of the confiscated letters were forwarded to military or civilian authorities, so that they could take appropriate measures to maintain discipline and preserve law and order at home.

This accounts for the fact that some soldiers' letters (with or without official comments) found their way into the administrative files of the Kingdom of Westphalia. Portions of the archives of the kingdom fell into the possession of a general in Russian service and were eventually turned over to the Russian Government. At present they are deposited in the Manuscript Division of the Leningrad Public Library.

Mr. S. N. Iskiul'—senior researcher at the Leningrad Division of the Institute of History of the Academy of Sciences of the U.S.S.R.—has discovered the six letters translated below in the course of his work on Russian diplomacy with respect to the German states in the Napoleonic era. He has published them, in Russian, with his commentaries and notes, in *Osvoboditel'noe dvizhenie v Rossii* (The liberation movement in Russia), No. 7 (Saratov: University of Saratov), 1978, pp. 101–10. He has kindly provided me with a typed copy of the original German text. I am very grateful to him for allowing reproduction of this material. I have made use of his valuable commentaries and Russian translation for the introduction and to clarify some obscure passages. In my own translation, I have attempted to convey not only the meaning but also the manner of writing and the uneducated flavor of these letters, which have an immediacy that memoirs written years after the events do not have as a rule. We have no information on either the background or the fate of the authors—they speak for the suffering, faceless common people.

I

Written in camp, 9 June 1812

To the Master craftsman Figner in Eisleben

*M*ost *beloved parents, Father and Mother. If this small letter of mine reaches you still in good health it will be a heartfelt pleasure for me. As to myself, I am, thank God, so far still quite fresh and healthy, and, dear parents, that I could not write you earlier has saddened me much.*

But, dear parents and good friends, if I am to write you of my present condition, how pitifully I am faring, me and my comrades, it is not to be described. God would soon take pity and give us, poor folk, soon again rest and peace.

Now, dear parents, as I have so pitifully kept my Easter and Pentecost, so did the poorest man on earth have it better than me and many. For Pentecost we had so little to live on that me had not half a pound of bread in three days. It would have been the same if we had had more, for it was too little to fill one and too much to starve, for we received no meat nor vegetables; so that from hunger thirty men killed ourselves a dog and have picked nettles and have cooked us a greenery dish with the dog's fat [as shortening] and eaten the meat for much hunger, for in the Polish lands there is so little to live on, that it would be little wonder if one would at the end starve to death, for bread, beer, and brandy is so expensive that our five days' pay could be used up in half an hour and [still] not know whether one has eaten or not. I get every five days six good pennies [Groschen].[1] If at home in Eisleben me buys for one Groschen spirits or liquor [Schnaps], me gets more for it than for twenty farthings [Kreuzer] in Poland, bread and beer. At that, the beer is as bad as the worst in Eisleben. We stand now not far from the Russian border in camp, where we arrived 5 June at twelve o'clock of the night and expect to see the enemy any day and hour. We are from home at least 160 miles away. Now then, dear parents and good friends, if I may ask you if it is possible to help me out with a little money so that I can still the great hunger, and should I return home I'll know how to thank you, so help me God on Judgment Day. Dear Father and Mother, be so kind to give a greeting to Louise Dordner from her brothers, they both are still quite hale and healthy and they are as pitiful as I am. We are together in camp with the 1st Division, 2nd Brigade. I am still with the 3rd Line Regiment, 2nd Battalion of the Grenadier Company and Louise Dordner's brothers are with the 2nd Regiment, 2nd Battalion of the Voltigeur Company.

Fare well you all and I would wish that this letter not be the last. I remain your faithful son unto death.

WILHELM FIGNER

[On the side added] Dear parents, don't take it amiss that the letter is so poorly written, it was [written] on the ground. But if you write to me you must write to 3rd Regiment, 2nd Battalion Grenadier Company to Westphalian Army in Poland.

II

To the Widow of Mr. Herrman
Kunkel, Marburg, Kingdom of
Westphalia

Russian Poland, Grodno, 16 July 1812

Y*our dear letter from last month arrived properly
in Warsaw, however, the one you sent to Mr.
Lieutenant Kessmann I did not receive, it must
have gotten lost. Not I am in Russia where it is
worse for me than in the other Poland.*[1] *Here
there is a lack of all foodstuffs. The bread that
is delivered is so bad that one can't eat it, yet very
dear to buy, one bread is paid eight pennies*
[Groschen], *it is baked from chaff and at that it is not baked through, it lies
like lead on the stomach. Hunger drives it down though. Meat is also very bad,
half smelly, and yet it has to be eaten. What else can one eat? Our march from
Warsaw to here was good and bad, we quartered under the free sky, God was
our host. Thunderstorm rains have at times drenched us thoroughly. For four days
I did not have a single dry thread on me and then nothing in the belly but a gulp
of wutki* [vodka] *and a piece of dark bread* [Pomzernickel, *i.e.,* Pumpernickel].
We marched with the King [of Westphalia] *without rest, ten to sixteen hours a
day on horseback. Of rivers we crossed the Narwa* [actually the Warthe], *Narev,
Bug and now we are across the Niemen in Russian Poland. There were ten
regiments of Cossacks in this town, but they have been expelled by the Polish
army while the Cossacks burned down the bridges behind themselves.*[2] *One hundred
Cossacks were taken prisoner, many died. The captured Cossacks were all pitifully
dressed, poorly armed. They must have been irregulars. One can't go far from
the town, there is always some of this riffraff around. The Russians have retreated
a lot. The*[ir] *army stands far from here. Our army follows on their heels. The
headquarters of Emperor Napoleon is in Wilno, so far did the French army*

advance. There will be a major battle these days. Tomorrow our march resumes with the King. This town greeted the King with all expressions of honor and swore fealty to Napoleon. Our good life has ended since we left Warsaw. Now one has to learn to suffer hunger and thirst. Our faces look different. Brown in the face like a chestnut and a mustache under my nose have completely disfigured me. Thank God I am in health, I bite at times in the old army bread, so that it rattles, and drive the hunger away. I could not get any money from Dr. Dieffenbach, for he has none, he would have gladly obliged me if he had not given all his cash against a remittance through a good friend. I am now so broke that I have no money to make myself shirts. I don't know what to do. Today I'll speak again to our doctor, if he has none [money] I'll go immediately to Nan at the field post [office] if he can't lend me money. It would be good if you would immediately speak with his parents and pay them the money. You have to ask them to write him that if I have money needs he should lend me [some]. I have to have two louis d'or to pay off my debts to my comrades and buy myself three shirts or have them made.[3] One louis d'or can't help me at all, I got too broke on the march to pay everything with one louis d'or. If I can hunt up money today I'll let you know and will put a note with the letter for your guidance. I greet my brothers and sisters. Farewell and stay nicely in health.

KUNKEL

III

*D*ear Mother,
I am forced not to send off this letter yet for lack
of time. We had to march off from Grodno in a
hurry and made a big march. The Russians are
pushed back and soon there will be fought a major
battle. Until now there were only avant-garde
skirmishes at which several Cossacks were left
dead, the streets are full of horses that died or
were killed. Dr. Dieffenbach cannot give me money for he has not gotten his pay.
Send me right away two louis d'or so that I can soon be free [of need]. It goes
very bad for me, it cannot last longer this way. There is no pay either, not much
to live on, so one has to go hungry. You pay these two louis d'or at the post,
you get a receipt for it that you send me in a letter. I receive thus the money
without trouble at the army, it has to be done right away or much time is lost
and I have to wait that much longer. This letter will get fast to Cassel through
an opportunity with the former garde du corps Schmidt. *Keep well. I am still*
healthy.

HER[MANN?] KUNKEL

IV

To Johannes Heit [?]
Spangenberg in Westphalia
Department of Werra

*B*est mother, sisters, brother-in-law, and friends!
   It is time at long last that I write to you,
my best ones. Duty demanded it long ago but I
wanted to get over the danger that I have now
gotten over. I am—after a light leg wound which
I received on 7 September near Musii in the major
battle from a bullet on the right leg—healthy and
sprightly. It was also a light wound, I could walk
again in eight days, but many of my comrades had to leave their lives, but we
have always stayed in possession of the battlefield and got the victory. Now we
are stationed here and no one knows what is going on. Cattle barns are our
quarters, where we bustle about in manure and dirt like pigs. It is very cold here
already and many die of a natural death, few of us will be lucky to step again
onto Germany. I hope, with God's help, to return to you, it is as if an unseen
power wants to preserve me, for so many comrades around me have been killed
and wounded, only I have come through unscathed, except for the small wound
as said before.

   I know nothing about peace to write you. Everything is exaggeratedly
expensive, bread that costs three pennies [Groschen] at home costs here Thaler
18 Groschen—also 2 Thaler. How often do I think of your potatoes that we
don't have at all. Now we learn well to appreciate their value.[1] I wish nothing
more than to eat one every eight days. When I return to you some day I will tell
you more. I only wish that you stay in health that long [i.e., until then].

   Dear Mother, go to Elhardorf to Hossfeld's parents and tell them that he *is still in good health and that he greets them. You [and they] can write together as I am his sergeant.*

I have heard that Hossbach is in the hospital. Vockeroth is still in good health, I spoke to him a few days ago. Kratzenberg from Mannscheid has lost his left thumb. I have more to write but now it is not proper. Now I have to remind you that you should tell my brother and sister-in-law that I received their letter, would have replied if I had not written to the brothers-in-law Spintler and Schirholtz and transmitted greetings each time. If you'd send my brother the whole letter you'd do me a great favor, for to write many letters would cost you too much as I can't pay anything.[2] We don't get any pay anymore. Greet all my friends and former comrades. To you, dear parents, thousand greetings from your faithful

Farewell and write soon.

H. ESCHRATH

Mazaik [Mozhaisk] 13 October 1812

*To the Master Stonemason
Wärncke in the town of
Mannsfeld, Department of Saale*

Greetings in God, much beloved parents. If my small letter finds you in good health I should be mightily glad. What concerns me, I am pretty much in health. Here in the white country we'll have to die all of hunger. All is burnt and the Russian [army] has carried off all subjects [inhabitants], as they had such a fear of us, and there is no food to be found because nobody is to be found in any town. Whenver a house is found it is empty and dark. Now, dear parents, I will complain of my circumstances as it was for us in three battles; 16 August before Smolensk Fortress, that was the first, the second was 19 August again two miles from Smolensk. Here they [Russians] stood again their ground. But they were again trounced [?]. In both battles did the Good Lord help me [stay] without a wound while I had to see so many [of my] countrymen fall, with arms and legs shot off, the way I saw little Selter lie on the battlefield. The third battle was on 7 September near Ziassko, which lasted three days. But the Westphalians were in the front lines for only one day, but in the sourest ride to where the Russians had entrenched themselves. But we beat them again. But we are now a small army. The regiment is now about 400 men strong, as it came out of the fire, not counting those who are now dying of hunger and lie under the open sky though it is already so cold.

Dear parents, now I have to give news of our last battle, as we had already gone hungry for three days and marched day and night, at five in the morning we marched into this battle with a cabbage stump [in the stomach] and we were in *it until nine in the evening. And then we again had nothing and could not eat for tiredness. A sutler came along, he had brandy, I still had three twenty-penny pieces in my possession, I gave them for a little brandy that picked me up, otherwise I too wouldn't be of this world. You can easily imagine how many people have remained [on the battlefield] so that we could not drink water [?] anymore.*[1] *Only cannon fire from morning to evening. God has helped me out of the third battle also without harm, though the bullets hailed down pretty well, as if one were to take peas and throw them at someone. But none got me. Stackelberg and Zeinert did not see anything of all our battles, for their regiment remained at rest. Stutz and Gutwasser went to the hospital as it was going to start soon. Fritze Bär is gone, Grosche from Jorenzen and the little Selter from Bentorff [also]. I can't give any news of the others. Denckwitz is also supposed to be dead his sergeant told me. I can't write anything for sure, but he is not to be found at the regiment. They are only 150 men strong, the whole cavalry is lost. Now I want to write you about the Russian town of misery—Moscow—which is seven hours' [walk] long and as wide, and the Russians put fire to it. For four hours it burned and then it was extinguished. And we were stationed before Moscow and Mozhaisk and don't know whether we are going forward or back. There is a cease-fire now—7 October there was again a battle behind Moscow. There the Russians were all scattered again. On the eighth a cease-fire was made again. One more thing, much beloved parents, I received the last letter on the morning after the battle, that was 20 August, and I was much gladdened that I came safe and out of the fire and the letter arrived well. Dear parents, you wrote me about my brother Friedrich concerning the soldiers [i.e., his being called up]. There I can't do anything just now. The major has replied to me that they [authorities?] know that I am [at the Army] and bring letters from me that I am in Russia 400 miles away. And one can't write much [from] here. Sending [the letter] takes a long time. Moreover should something happen [to me?] call that to their attention and they will release him.*[2] *I don't know what else to write except that you will shortly see many cripples without arm and leg and so many must die pitifully of hunger and terrible dangers. Russians appear all the time for the last battle. Let's end now. Finally farewell and stay healthy until we speak again. And I expect an answer again. Many greetings to brothers and sisters, brothers-in-law and sister-in-law, to the Baltzens and Krögens and all good friends and acquaintances. And I am quite well if I only can live [word illegible]. Farewell. I remain your faithful son until death.*

JOHANN ANDREAS WÄRNCKE

VI

*D*earest parents!

 You will forgive that I did not write for so long, for circumstances have not permitted it earlier. Dear parents, I wrote you from Thorn but since I did not get an answer and since I could not stay longer and we fast marched away in the direction of Riga where we were stationed one month with the field bakery; our corps was ordered to Moscow and the French troops beat back the Russians and we occupied Moscow. Unfortunately we were there only twenty-four hours as the Russian troops pushed forward again and put fire to this city, with grenades and incendiary bombs was this beautiful city destroyed and turned into an ash heap. And so we retreated, when many died and I lost my health. We retreated twenty-four miles when Emperor Alexander encircled us with 200,000 in our back and captured us. Whoever did not die was taken prisoner. Dear parents, if I had been with the Westphalian or Saxon army I would have kept my own. However, to [my] misfortune I was with the corps of the Prince of Eckmühl[1] in the bakery so that they [Russians] did not leave a shirt on our skin. So you can well imagine, dear parents, in what condition I am in. I would like dutifully to ask whether you could help me out with some shirts. Dear parents, one more thing I wish, I would very much like to know how it is with your respective health. More I don't know to write you but I would like to know what my Miss Waase is doing and my cousin Heinrich. More I don't wish anything, but to have detailed news of both as soon as possible. More I don't know what to write than that you will soon get foreign troops. *Greet many times Sophie Lindick on the farm. The same of neighbor Peligen. Also here in Landsberg there came a battalion of the 3rd Westphalian Line Regiment midst whom I met two good friends named Christoph Calmes and Schluter give regards to their parents from both of them, you can imagine what joy this was. I don't know what more to write you except that I am your obedient son.*

GEORGE BORMANN

Address: The Peasant Inn. Landsberg on the Warthe

Notes to the Letters

I

1. "Good pennies" means coins having full value—a *Groschen* was worth one hundredth of a *Thaler*.

II

1. "Other Poland" refers to Prussian Poland.

2. Napoleon, hoping to have the collaboration and support of the Poles, set up the Grand Duchy of Warsaw and recruited from the population. The Polish Corps was under the command of Prince Poniatowski.

3. Louis d'or—a gold coin, originally minted in France with a representation of the French king on it, hence the name. It was worth twenty francs.

IV

1. Implies that the potato was still a novelty in Westphalia and its consumption resisted.

2. Postage could be prepaid or, more frequently, it had to be paid for by the recipient.

V

1. Probably he means that the great number of dead bodies on the battlefield, left without burial, contaminated wells and streams.

2. The context suggests that his brother was being called up while a son of the family was already serving in the Army. Letters from Russia were to be proof of his campaign service, and the wounding of a brother (or his death in battle) freed one from being called up.

VI

1. Prince d'Eckmühl was the title of Louis Nicolas Davout, able marshal of Napoleon.

About the Illustrations

THE ILLUSTRATIONS REPRODUCED IN THIS volume are drawn from the Russian/Soviet and East European collections of the New York Public Library, and are meant to illustrate some of the places, personalities, and events described so vividly in Walter's diary.

The legend from each of the illustrations is translated into English, and the original sources identified.

—E. Kasinec and R. H. Davis, Jr.

Borck, C. F. W. *Napoleon's Erster Traum in Moskwa* [Napoleon's First Dream in Moscow]. St. Petersburg: Iwan Glazunow [sic: Glazunov], 1812. *Plate 13.*

The Library's copy bears the bookstamp of the Russian Imperial Palace Library at Tsarskoe Selo.

Borst, Otto. *Alte Städte in Württemberg* [The Old Cities in Württemberg]. Munich: Prestel Verlag, 1968. *Plates 1, 2.*

Bulgakov. *Ruskiye i Napoleon Bonaparte* [*The Russians and Napoleon Bonaparte*]. *Pokhod rossiiskikh i soiuznykh voisk v Germaniiu i Frantsiiu. V 1813 i v nachale 1814 goda. Chast' pervaia. Ot perekhoda Rossiiskikh voisk za granitsu, do zakliucheniia peremiriia. Izd. vtoroe.* [The campaign of Russian and allied troops to Germany and France. In 1813 and the beginning of 1814. Part One. From the crossing of the border by Russian troops until the conclusion of the truce. Second edition.] Moscow: Tip. S. Silivanovskago [sic: Selivanovskago], 1814. *Plate 11.*

Bulgakov was a diplomat and high-ranking Imperial official. The Library's copy of Bulgakov (see Moskovskii Zhitel, below) bears the ex libris of P. A. Efremov (1830–1907), the noted bibliographer and bibliophile, and at some point passed through the well-known St. Petersburg antiquarian bookstore of V. I. Klochkov (1862–1915).

Faber du Faur. *Blätter aus meinem Portefeuille* [Leaves from My Portfolio] [1831– 43]. *Plates 3–9, 16–19.*

Drawings of the French campaign are by the artist Faber du Faur, published by F. Autenrieth of Stuttgart. The Library's volume of plates was originally in the collections of the Museum Library in Ludwigsburg, and bears its bookstamp.

Hess, Peter von. *Illiustrirovannaia otechestvennaia voina 1812 g.* [The War of 1812 in Illustrations]. St. Petersburg: Tip. F. S. Sushchinskago, 1887. *Plate 10.*

Photoengraved by I. Goffert from a painting by P. von Hess (1792–1871). This photoengraving was published by the firm of Shere-Nabgol'ts and Company in Moscow.

Moskovskii Zhitel [A Moscow Resident, i.e., Bulgakov, A. Ia.]. *Ruskiye i Napoleon Bonaparte . . .* Izd. vtoroe. [The Russians and Napoleon Bonaparte . . . Second edition.] Moscow: Tip. S. Selivanovskago, 1813. *Plate 12.*

This earlier, variant edition of Bulgakov (see above) is bound in a fine presentation binding, stamped in small letters with the names of the artists. Purchased by New York antiquarian bookdealer Simeon A. Bolan in 1935, like many volumes in the NYPL, it was most probably of Imperial provenance.

Mundt, Albert (ed.). *Die Freiheitskriege in Bildern* [The Wars of Liberation in Pictures]. Munich/Leipzig: Einhorn Verlag, 1913. *Chapter headpieces.*

The illustrations that appear at the opening of each section depict the retreat of wounded and maimed French soldiers. The illustrations were made on the spot by C. G. H. Geissler, and are now in the collections of the State Historical Museum in Leipzig.

[Pöhlmann, J. P.]. *Die Kosacken: Oder Historische Darstellung . . .* [The Cossacks: Or Their Historical Formation . . .]. Vienna and Prague: Joseph Feldner, [1812]. *Plate 15.*

Springer, Otto, ed. and trans. *A German Conscript with Napoleon: Jakob Walter's Recollections of the Campaigns of 1806–1807, 1809, and 1812–1813.* In *Bulletin of the University of Kansas,* vol. 6, no. 3. Lawrence, Kans., 1938. *Frontispiece.*

Terebenev, I. "Ugoshchenie Napoleonu v Rossii" ["An offering to Napoleon in Russia"]. *Karrikatury Napoleona I* [Caricatures of Napoleon I]. [n.p., n.d.] Printed and engraved by Miterebenov. *Plate 14.*

This engraving is also reproduced in Dmitrii A. Rovinskii's *Russkie narodnye kartinki* [Russian popular prints], vol. 2. St. Petersburg, 1881–93.

Chronology

RULERS AND REGIMES

FRANCE

1774–92	Louis XVI
1792–95	National Convention (Convention Nationale)
1795–99	Directory (Directoire)
1799–1804	Consulate
1804–14/15	Napoleon I, Emperor of the French
1814/1815–24	Louis XVIII

RUSSIA

1762–96	Catherine II
1796–1801	Paul I
1801–25	Alexander I

HOLY ROMAN EMPIRE AND AUSTRIA

1780–90	Joseph II, Emperor of Holy Roman Empire of the Germanic Nation, Duke of Austria
1790–92	Leopold II (same as above)
1792–1835	Francis II, Emperor of Holy Roman Empire and Duke of Austria until 1804; Emperor of Holy Roman Empire and of Austria, 1804–6; Emperor of Austria, 1804–35

PRUSSIA

1786–97	Frederick William II
1797–1840	Frederick William III

160

ENGLAND

1760–1820	George III (from 1811 until his death, his son, later George IV, acted as regent)
1783–1801, 1804–6	William Pitt the Younger, Prime Minister

WÜRTTEMBERG

1797–1816	Friedrich II
1816–64	Wilhelm I

Main Events in Europe

1789 5 May Convocation of Estates General

14 July Storming of Bastille

4 August Abolition of feudal rights and privileges

27 August Declaration of the Rights of Man and of the Citizen

1792–97   War of the First Coalition

1792 20 April Declaration of war on Austria

20 September Battle of Valmy—French repulse the invasion

6 November Battle of Jemappes—Austrians evacuate Belgium

19 November Proclamation promising liberation of peoples from monarchical tyranny

1793–94   Reign of Terror

1793 23 August Universal levy of male population—creation of the "nation in arms"

19 December Lifting of siege of Toulon by English navy—Bonaparte earns his first laurels (born on 15 August 1769 at Ajaccio in Corsica)

1795 Proclamation of Batavian Republic

5 March Treaty of Basel—Prussia withdraws from war

1796–97   Bonaparte's Italian campaign—victories of Lodi, Arcola, Rivoli—proclamation of Lombard Republic

1797 18 April Preliminaries of peace at Leoben with Austria

9 July Proclamation of Cisalpine Republic

17 October Treaty of Campo Formio—Austria concedes French acquisitions

1798–99   Bonaparte in Egypt

1798–1801   War of the Second Coalition

1798	9 November	Bonaparte's coup d'état—proclaimed First Consul (18 Brumaire, according to revolutionary calendar)

1798 9 November Bonaparte's coup d'état—proclaimed First Consul
        (18 Brumaire, according to revolutionary calendar)

1801 9 February Treaty of Lunéville with Austria

1802 27 March Treaty of Amiens with England

   18 May Creation of the Légion d'honneur

   2 August Bonaparte proclaimed Consul for life

1804 18 May Bonaparte proclaims himself Emperor of the French

   2 December Coronation of Napoleon as emperor

1805 Third Coalition formed against France

   21 October Battle of Trafalgar

   2 December Battle of Austerlitz

   26 December Treaty of Pressburg with Austria

1806–7 War with Prussia and Russia

1806–12 War between Turkey and Russia

1806 12 July Confederation of the Rhine formed

   6 August Holy Roman Empire of the Germanic Nation dissolved

   14 October Battles of Jena and Auerstädt—Berlin occupied by French

   21 November Decree of Berlin instituting Continental Blockade

1807–11 Reforms in Prussia

1807 7–8 February Battle of Eylau

   14 June Battle of Friedland

   7–9 July Treaties of Tilsit with Prussia and Russia

1808–9 Russo-Swedish War—Russia conquers Finland

1808–14 Napoleon's war in Spain

1809–10 Tyrolean rebellion

1809 War with Austria

   5–6 July Battle of Wagram

   14 October Treaty of Schönbrunn with Austria

1810 April Napoleon marries Archduchess Marie Louise of Austria

1812 28 May Treaty of Bucharest ending Russo-Turkish war

   24–26 June Napoleon crosses Niemen River

   17–18 August Battle of Smolensk

   7 September Battle of Borodino (or of the Moskova)

   14 September Moscow occupied by Grande Armée

   15–19 September Fire devastates Moscow

   19 October Napoleon orders retreat

24 October Battle of Maloiaroslavets

26–28 November Grande Armée recrosses Berezina River

1813 3 February Appeal by Prussia to rise against Napoleon

28 February Convention of Kalisch between Russia and Prussia to carry on war against Napoleon

17 March Organization of Landsturm and Landwehr in Prussia and German lands

12 August Austria reenters war against France

9 September Treaty of Teplitz—Austria, Prussia, and Russia agree to fight France to victory

16–19 September Battle of Leipzig

1814 9 March Treaty of Chaumont—Four-power treaty setting up Quadruple Alliance of England, Austria, Russia, and Prussia

31 March Allies enter Paris

11 April Napoleon abdicates—goes into exile to island of Elba

30 May First Treaty of Paris

September 1814–June 1815 Congress of Vienna

1815 20 March–29 June The Hundred Days

18 June Battle of Waterloo

22 June Second abdication of Napleon—eventually banned to island of St. Helena, where he died in 1821

7 July Second occupation of Paris and return of Louis XVIII

1815 26 September Conclusion of Holy Alliance

20 November Second Peace Treaty of Paris—Renewal of Quadruple Alliance

Place Names

The names are first given as they appear in the text of Walter's autobiography. Alternative spellings and designations are given to facilitate their identification on more recent maps.

The distances indicated are approximate and largely culled from the notes in the original publication, *Bulletin of the University of Kansas—Humanistic Studies*, vol. VI, no. 3 (Lawrence, Kans.: University of Kansas, Department of Journalism Press, 1938). In some cases, especially in East Prussia, places could not be identified since there has been a radical renaming since 1945.

Adlerberg territory—see Vorarlberg

Altdorf—now Weingarten

Altshausen—40 km N of Lake Constance

Ansbach—40 km SW of Nuremberg

Asperg—Asberg—5 km E of Ludwigsburg, 10 km NW of Stuttgart

Baltic Sea

Bayreuth—in Bavaria, Upper Franconia

Beeskow on the Spree—Brandenburg province, 40 km SW of Frankfurt-on-the-Oder

Belgard—Białogard—Pomerania, now Poland, 35 km SE of Colberg

Beresina—Berezina—river, E of Minsk

Berlin—capital of Prussia

Bernlohhof—Bernlohöf—hamlet 15 km S. of Ellwangen

Beshenkovichi—35 km SW of Vitebsk

Biberach—in Württemberg, 100 km SE of Stuttgart

Bischofstein—East Prussia, SW of Königsberg

Bobr—190 km W of Smolensk

Borissov—Borisov—75 km NE of Minsk

Borodino—hamlet on confluent of Kolocha and Moskva rivers, 110 km W of Moscow

Borovsk—20 km N of Malo Jaroslavetz

Brandenburg—province of Prussia, also provincial town

Braslav—50 km SE of Dvinsk

Bregenz—on Lake Constance in Austrian Tyrol

Breslau—Wrocław—capital of Silesia, now Poland

Buchhorn—now Friedrichshafen on Lake Constance

Bug—river in Poland

Bunzlau—in Silesia, 35 km WNW of Liegnitz

Calw—Kalw—in Württemberg, 30 km SW of Stuttgart

Cassel—Kassel—in Hessen, Germany

Colberg—Kolberg—Kołobrzeg—in Pomerania, now Poland

Constance, Lake of—Bodensee—between Switzerland, Austria, and Germany

Crossen—Krossen—45 km SE from Frankfurt-on-the-Oder in Brandenburg

Dam—Altdamm—village 5 km ESE of Stettin, Pomerania, now Poland

Danzig—Gdańsk, 274 km NW of Warsaw

Darkehmen—East Prussia, SE of Königsberg

Diescony—village, see Labonary

Dinkelsbühl—Bavaria, 20 km NE of Ellwangen

Disna—30 km W of Polotsk

Dnieper—Dnepr—river in U.S.S.R.

Dornbirn—in Austrian Vorarlberg, 13 km S of Bregenz

Dorogobush—Dorogobuzh—75 km ENE of Smolensk

Dresden—capital of Saxony

Drysviaty—Drisviaty—between Vilna and Dvina River

Dubrovna—W of Smolensk—75 km NNE of Mohilev on the Dnieper

Dvina—Dünau—river in Latvia

Dvinsk—Dünaburg—Daugavpils—in Lithuania

Eisleben—in Anhalt, 60 km NW of Leipzig

Elbe—river in Germany

Elhardorf?

Ellwangen on the Jagst—in Württemberg, 60 km ENE of Stuttgart

Eve—village between Kovno and Vilna

Frankenstein—in Prussian Silesia, 50 km E of Berlin

Frankfort-on-the-Oder—Frankfurt-on-the-Oder—in Posen province of Prussia

Fraustadt—in Posen province

Fürstenwalde—in Brandenburg, 50 km E of Berlin

Galicia—province, formerly part of Austrian Poland, now U.S.S.R.

Glatz—Kłodzko—Silesia, on Neisse River, 80 km S of Breslau

Gnesen—Gniezno—in Prussian Poland, 45 km E of Posen

Grodno—Byelorussian S.S.R., 150 km SW of Vilna

Grossglogau—fortress on Oder in Silesia, 60 km WNW of Breslau—also known
   as Glogau—Głogòw

Gshatsk—Gzhatsk—150 km WSW of Moscow

Hechingen—55 km S of Stuttgart

Hochkirch—village, now in Poland

Hofen—combined with Buchhorn to form Friedrichshafen on Lake Constance

Hohenberg—village, 7.5 km NW of Ellwangen

Inowrazlav—Inowrocław—between Gnesen and Thorn

Isny—80 km SE of Ulm in Bavaria

Kalisch—Kalisz—200 km WSW of Warsaw

Kaluga—175 km SWS of Moscow

Kalvaria—Kalvariya—180 km ESE of Königsberg

Kempten—60 km E of Friedrichshafen on Lake Constance

Killerthal—valley of Starzel River, S of Tübingen, Württemberg

Kochanova—Kokhanovo—140 km W of Smolensk

Königsberg—Kaliningrad—capital of East Prussia, now U.S.S.R.

Kosatschisna—Karachisno—village between Vilna and Dvina River

Kovno—Kowno—Kaunas—Lithuania, its capital from 1920 to 1940

Krasnoë—30 km WSW of Smolensk

Kremlin—fortress and palace section of Moscow

Krupky—Krupki—195 km W of Smolensk

Künzelsau—35 km NE of Heilbronn, Württemberg

Labonary—Diescony?—village between Vilna and Dvina River

Lagarben—Laggarben—Lamgarben—East Prussia, S of Königsberg

Landsberg on the Warthe—Gorzòw Wielkopolske—140 km E of Berlin

Leipsic—Leipzig—major city in Saxony

Liecnize—Loshnitsa?—near Bobr

Lindau—on Lake Constance, 20 km E of Friedrichshafen

Löventin—village in East Prussia, S of Königsberg

Ludwigsburg—royal residence, 9 km N of Stuttgart

Main—river, Germany

Maliaty—N of Vilna, E of Vilkomirz

Malo Jaroslavetz—Maloiaroslavets—110 km SWS of Moscow

Marburg—in Hessen, Germany

Mariampol—Mariyampole—50 km NE of Suwałki

Marmsfeld?

Memel—Niemań—Nemunas—river in Lithuania and Byelorussian S.S.R.

Mergentheim—in Württemberg, 90 km NE of Stuttgart

Minsk—in Byelorussian S.S.R., 250 km W of Smolensk

Moldavia—province, formerly in Ottoman Empire, then Romania, now in U.S.S.R.

Molodetschno—Molodechno—100 km SE of Vilna

Moscow—Moskva—capital of Russia and U.S.S.R.

Moshaisk—Mozhaisk—Mazaik—120 km W of Moscow

Moskva—river flowing through Moscow, tributary of Oka and Volga

Narev—Narew—Narwa—river in Poland

Neeswicz—perhaps Nezvizh—SSW of Minsk

Neglinnaia—rivulet, tributary of Moskva River at the Kremlin, now covered over

Neisse—Nisa—on Klodzka River, in Silesia, now Poland

Niemen—river, see Memel

Niklawi—Mlava?—Mława?—110 km NNW of Warsaw

Nordenburg—East Prussia, 75 km SE of Königsberg

Nuremberg—Nürnberg—in Bavaria

Oder—Odra—river, now border of Poland on the west

Oehringen—20 km NE of Heilbronn

Orscha—Orsha—100 km W of Smolensk

Ortelsburg—East Prussia, 120 km SES of Königsberg

Ostrovno—village near Vitebsk

Plauen—in Saxony, 90 km SW of Leipzig

Plechnizi—Pleshchenitsy—75 km NE of Minsk, 40 km from Borissov

Plock—Plotsk—100 km WNW of Warsaw

Polotsk—Polock—on Dvina River, Byelorussian S.S.R.

Pomerania—province of Prussia, now Poland

Poniemon—Panemune—SE of Kovno on Niemen River

Posen—Poznań—midway between Berlin and Warsaw in former Prussian Poland

Prussia—kingdom

Ravensburg—20 km N of Friedrichshafen

Reichenbach—Silesia, 45 km SW of Breslau

Reppen—village in Brandenburg, 18 km E of Frankfurt-on-the-Oder

Rettstadt—5 km E of Ellwangen

Riga—capital of Lativian S.S.R.

Rosenberg—10 km NW of Ellwangen

Saale—river in Germany

St. Petersburg—Petrograd—Leningrad—captial of Russia from 1712 to 1918

Saulgau—55 km SE of Ulm in Bavaria

Saxe-Coburg—Sachsen-Koburg—former principality in Saxony

Saxe-Weimar—Sachsen-Weimar—former principality in Anhalt-Saxe

Saxony—Sachsen—formerly kingdom in Germany

Schorndorf—Württemberg, 25 km E of Stuttgart

Schweidnitz—Scheweinitz—Saxony, 65 km NE of Leipzig

Seeburg—East Prussia, SW of Königsberg

Selnia—river near Moscow

Sembin—Zembin—25 km NWN of Borissov

Semlevo—125 km NE of Smolensk

Silberberg—in Silesia, 50 km SE of Berlin

Silesia—Schlesien—province of kingdom of Prague

Slaiski—Seliche? Sedlicz?—between Minsk and Vilnius

Smolensk—capital of Byelorussian S.S.R.

Smorgoni—100 km NW of Minsk on road to Vilna

Spangenberg—S of Cassel

Stargard—in Pomerania, now Poland, 25 km ESE of Stettin

Stettin—Szczecin—on Oder, Pomerania, now Poland

Stuttgart—capital of Württemberg

Thorn—Toruń—200 km NW of Warsaw

Thuringia—Thüringen/Thuringian Forest—Thüringer Wald—mountainous district on border of Saxony

Toloczin—Tolochini—in Byelorussian S.S.R., 160 km W of Smolensk

Torgau—in Saxony, 50 km NE of Leipzig

Tyrol—Tirol—Southwestern province of Austria

Ula—Ulla—on Dvina River, 60 km W of Vitebsk

Vaihingen-on-the-Enz—22 km NW of Stuttgart

Vereia—Vereya—110 km WSW of Moscow, 20 km S of Moshaisk

Verina?

Viasma—Viazma—200 km W of Moscow

Vilkomirz—Wilkomierz—Ukmerge—75 km NW of Vilna

Vilna—Wilno—Vilno—Vilnius—capital of Lithuania

Vistula—Wisła—Weichsel—river in Poland

Vitebsk—in Byelorussian S.S.R.

Vorarlberg—mountainous massif in Western Tyrol on Swiss border

Waiblingen—10 km NE of Stuttgart

Waldenbuch—15 km SW of Stuttgart

Waldsee—35 km N of Friedrichshafen

Wangen—Württemberg, 75 km SW of Ulm

Warsaw—Warszawa—capital of Poland

Warthe—Warta—river in Germany and Poland

Weikersheim on Tauber—60 km N of Ellwangen

Weiltingen—20 km ENE of Ellwangen

Weimar—in Sachsen-Thüringen

Weingarten—monastery, 20 km N of Friedrichshafen

Werra—river in Germany

Westphalia—Westfalen—kingdom set up by Napoleon comprising several German territorial principalities

Württemberg—Württenberg—kingdom

Würzburg—in Bavaria

Wüstenroth—village, 20 km E of Heilbronn

Reading Suggestions

REFERENCE WORKS

Tulard, Jean. *Bibliographie critique des mémoires sur le consulat et l'empire écrits où traduits en francais.* Paris-Geneva: Librairie Droz, 1971. Most useful guide to memoir literature of the period.

———, ed. *Dictionnaire Napoléon.* Paris: Fayard, 1987. Most recent and up-to-date compendium, alphabetically arranged, on everything pertaining to Napoleon, his reign, wars, statecraft, and the major events of his day.

GENERAL HISTORIES OF THE PERIOD

Breunig, Charles. *The Age of Revolution and Reaction 1789–1850.* Vol. IV, *The Norton History of Modern Europe.* New York: W. W. Norton, 1970.

Gershoy, Leo. *The French Revolution and Napoleon.* New York: Appleton-Century-Crofts, 1955.

Holborn, Hajo. *A History of Modern Germany 1648–1840.* New York: Alfred A. Knopf, 1964.

Seton-Watson, Hugh. *The Russian Empire 1801–1917.* Oxford Clarendon Press, 1967.

Thomson, David. *Europe Since Napoleon.* New York: Alfred A. Knopf, 1957. Has useful survey account of Napoleonic period.

NAPOLEONIC WARS AND CAMPAIGN OF 1812

‡ Bourgogne, Adrien Jean Baptiste. *Memoirs of Sergeant Bourgogne 1812–1813.* Authorized translation with introduction by Hon. J. W. Fortescue. New York: Robert M. McBride, 1929.

‡ Brett-James, Antony, ed. *1812—Eyewitness Accounts of Napoleon's Defeat in Russia.* New York: St. Martin's Press, 1966.

‡ Caulaincourt, Armand Augustin Louis, marquis de, duc de Vicence. *Memoirs.* Edited by Jean Hanoteau, translation by Hamish Miles. London: Cassell, 1950.

‡ ———. *General Wilson's Journal 1812–1814.* London: William Kimber, 1964.

‡ Clausewitz, Carl von. *The Campaign of 1812 in Russia.* Translated from the German. London: J. Murray, 1843 (reprinted: Hattiesburg, Miss.: Academic International, 1970.)

‡ Coignet, J.R. *The Note-books of Captain Coignet, Soldier of the Empire.* London: Greenhill Books, 1985.

Duffy, Christopher. *Borodino and the War of 1812.* New York: Charles Scribner's Sons, 1973.

Josselson, Michael and Diana. *The Commander—A Life of Barclay de Tolly.* New York: Oxford University Press, 1980.

† Nafziger, George F. *Napoleon's Invasion of Russia.* Novato, Calif.: Presidio Press, 1988.

† Riehn, Richard K. *Napoleon's Russian Campaign.* New York: McGraw-Hill, 1990.

‡ Ségur, Paul Philippe. *Napoleon's Russian Campaign.* Boston: Houghton Mifflin, 1958.

Tarlé, E. V. *Napoleon's Invasion of Russia 1812.* New York, Toronto: Oxford University Press, 1942.

‡ Wilson, R. T., Sir. *Narrative of Events during the Invasion of Russia by Napoleon Bonaparte and the Retreat of the French Army 1812.* London: 1860.

Woloch, Isser. *The French Veteran from the Revolution to the Restoration.* Chapel Hill, N.C.: University of North Carolina Press, 1970.

And of course no one has surpassed Leo Tolstoy's description of the atmosphere in Russia during the Napoleonic period in *War and Peace.*

---

† Most recent professional accounts of the technical aspects of the campaign of 1812.

‡ Accounts by participants.

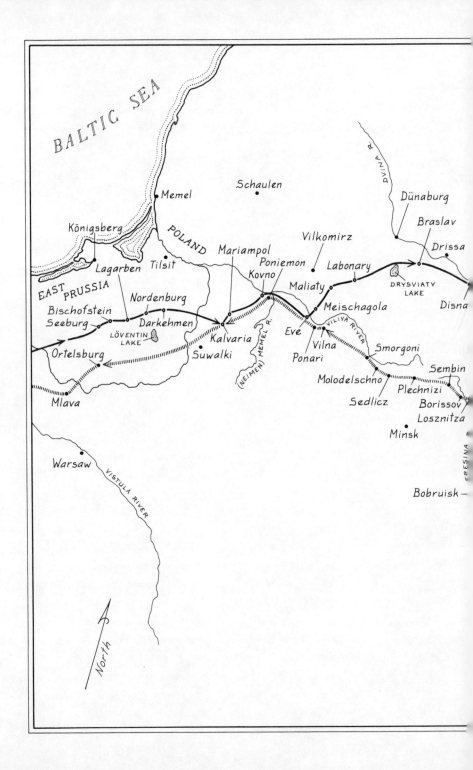